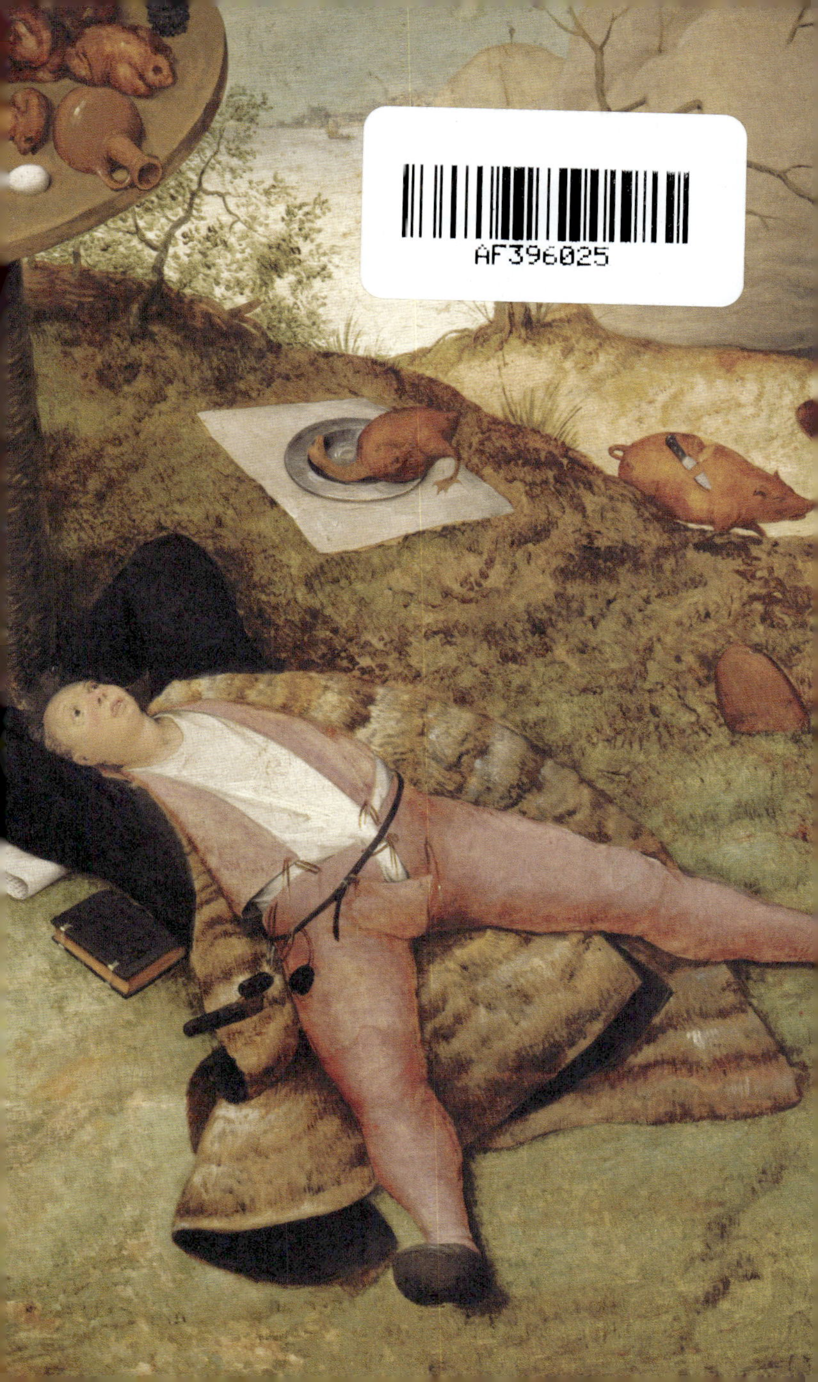
AF396025

T. J. Clark is Professor Emeritus of the History of Art at the University of California, Berkeley. He is the author of the seminal works *The Painting of Modern Life: Paris in the Art of Manet and His Followers* (1984) and *Farewell to an Idea: Episodes from a History of Modernism* (1999). He writes art criticism regularly for the *London Review of Books*. His other publications include *Image of the People: Gustave Courbet and the 1848 Revolution* (1983), *The Sight of Death* (2006), *Lowry and the Painting of Modern Life* (with Anne M. Wagner, accompanying a major Tate Britain exhibition, 2013), *Picasso and Truth: From Cubism to Guernica* (2013), *Heaven on Earth: Painting and the Life to Come* (2018), *If These Apples Should Fall: Cézanne and the Present* (2022) and *Those Passions: On Art and Politics* (2025).

POCKET PERSPECTIVES

Surprising, questioning, challenging, enriching: the Pocket Perspectives series presents timeless works by writers and thinkers who have shaped the conversation across the arts, visual culture and history. Celebrating the undiminished vitality of their ideas today, these covetable and collectable books embody the best of Thames & Hudson.

T.J. CLARK ON BRUEGEL

With 28 illustrations

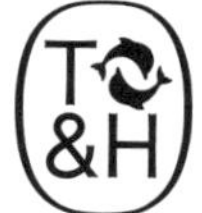

This book consists of an extract from *Heaven on Earth* by T. J. Clark, published by Thames & Hudson in 2018.

Front cover and endpapers: Details from Pieter Bruegel the Elder, *Land of Cockaigne*, 1567

First published in the United Kingdom in 2018 in *Heaven on Earth* by Thames & Hudson Ltd, 181A High Holborn, London WC1V 7QX

First published in the United States of America in 2018 in *Heaven on Earth* by Thames & Hudson Inc., 500 Fifth Avenue, New York, New York 10110

This abridged edition published in the United Kingdom in 2024 by Thames & Hudson Ltd, 181A High Holborn, London WC1V 7QX

This abridged edition published in the United States of America in 2024 Thames & Hudson Inc., 500 Fifth Avenue, New York, New York 10110

T. J. Clark on Bruegel
© 2024 Thames & Hudson Ltd, London
Text © 2018 T. J. Clark

British Library Cataloguing-in-Publication Data
A catalogue record for this book is available from the British Library

Library of Congress Control Number 2024935638

ISBN 978-0-500-02866-7

Printed in China by Shenzhen Reliance Printing Co. Ltd

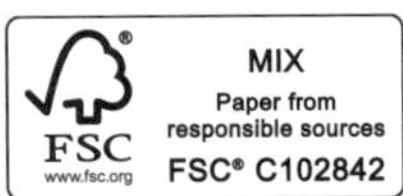

CONTENTS

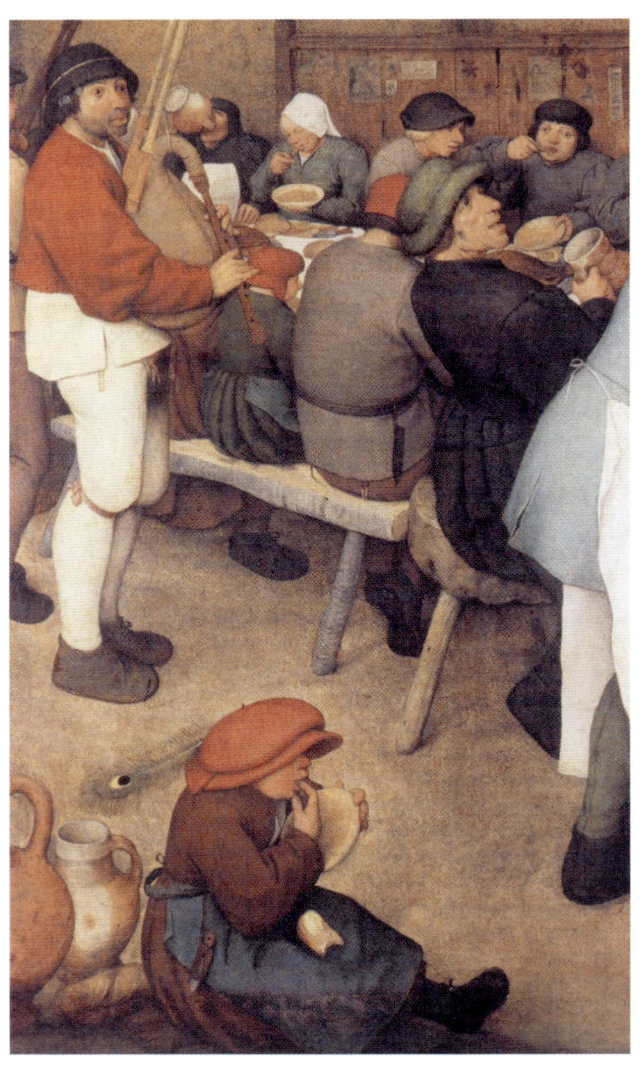

1. Pieter Bruegel the Elder,
Peasant Wedding, 1568, detail

BRUEGEL IN PARADISE

THE CLOSEST BRUEGEL ever came to painting the afterlife seems to have been in a mid-size panel, just over 20 inches high and 30 inches wide, called the *Land of Cockaigne*. The Dutch word for the place was *Luye-leckerlandt*, the hereafter as imagined by lazybones and gluttons. A certain amount is known about the hereafter's close German cousin, *Schlaraffenland*, which became a staple of early sixteenth-century chapbooks, intrigued by the idea's peasant origins and eager to moralize on the theme of eternity without effort.[1] There is a sense in the pamphlets, and perhaps in Bruegel's picture, that the idea is seen as 'medieval' – already looked back on from a leaner modernity.[2] Bruegel's panel is dated 1567: the same year as his *Conversion of Saint Paul*, that very modern subject, and in all likelihood the *Peasant Dance* and *Peasant Wedding*, now in Vienna. The child sucking its sticky fingers in *Peasant Wedding* is dreaming of a *Luye-leckerlandt* to come.

I began thinking about the *Land of Cockaigne* some years ago, mainly because of its treatment of gravity. Bruegel seemed to me a materialist, perhaps the deepest and most thoroughgoing to have left us a picture of the world; and in this he connected across history with

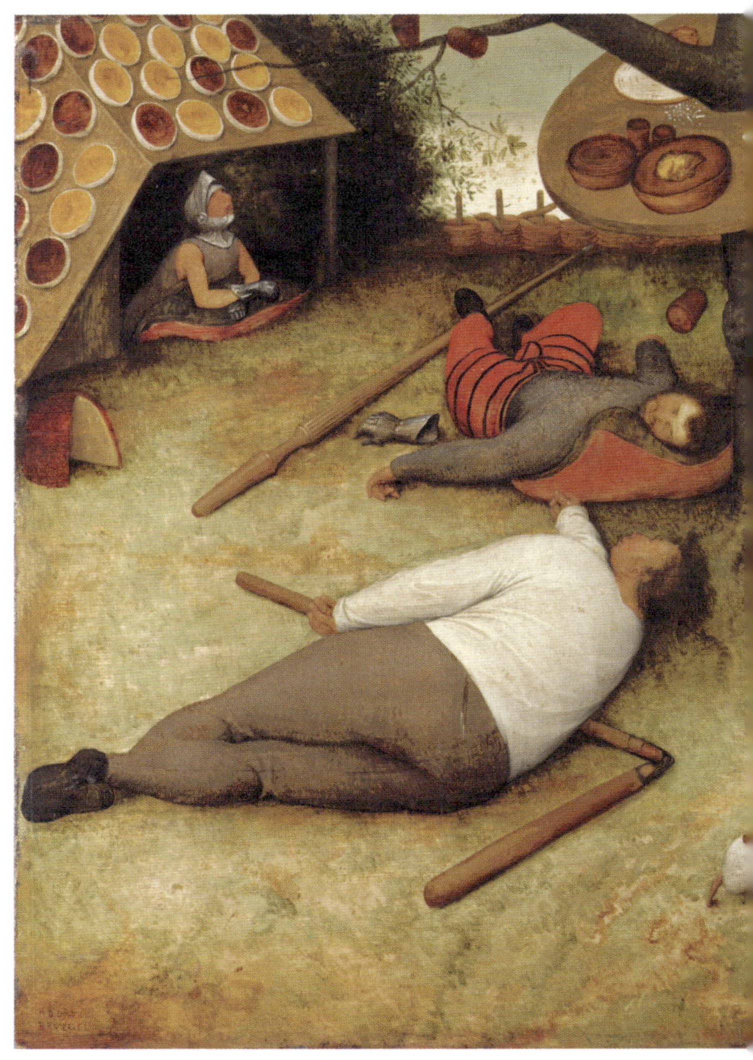

2. Pieter Bruegel the Elder,
Land of Cockaigne, 1567

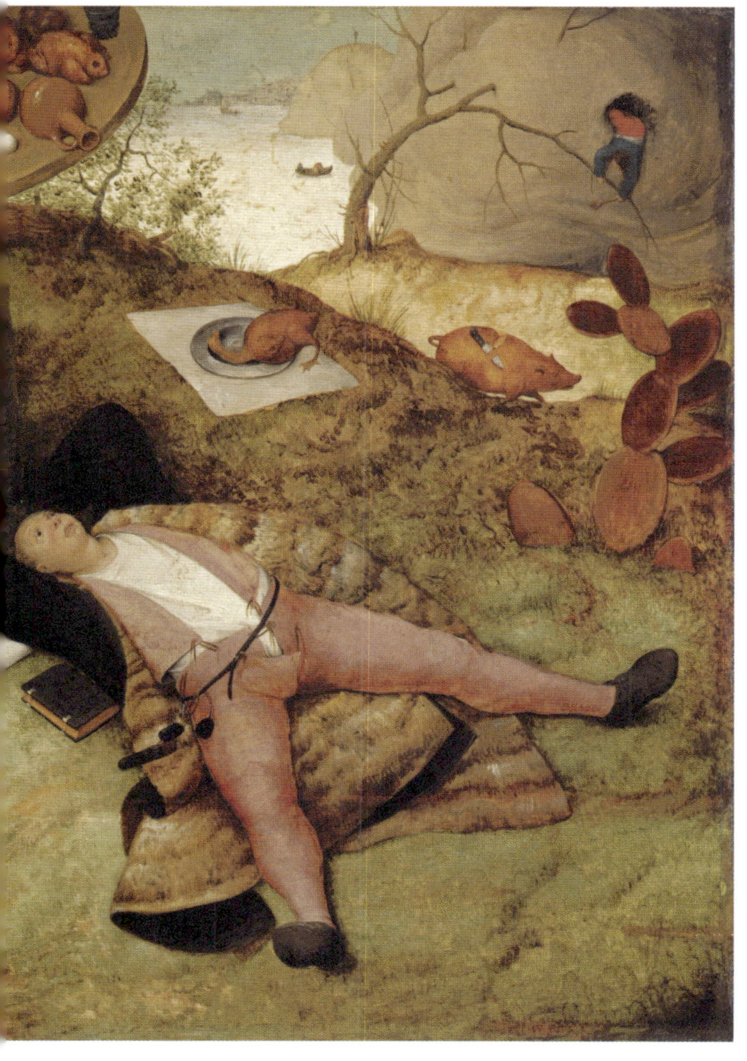

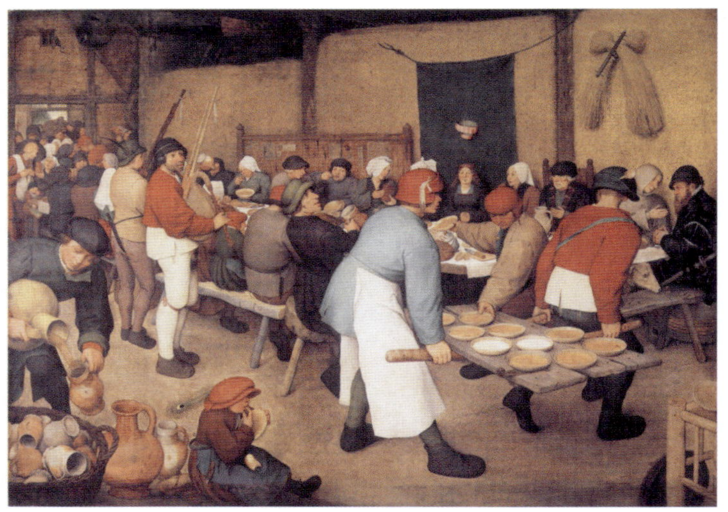

3. Pieter Bruegel the Elder,
Peasant Wedding, 1568

certain other painters – Poussin and Veronese chief among them – who had a similar interest in the human world's overall orientation, in particular the way the upright (or downfallen) body connected with the ground.[3] The fact of bipedalism was central to these artists' vision. This is not the place to explore the nature of such an interest more fully except to say that it strikes me as rare in painting, or rare in the sense that the interest shapes an artist's whole anthropology. One part of me finds the infrequency puzzling, since painting, of all the arts, seems in many ways best fitted to show how much of human nature and culture derives from uprightness – anatomical high standing – which the ground supports but at the same time qualifies. To be a little ominous about this, it surely mattered profoundly to the cultures from which Bruegel and Poussin emerged that human beings ended their days no longer vertical, and with the earth no longer their platform: 'Man comes and tills the earth and lies beneath.'[4] Some painters – surprisingly few, it emerges – make the contact of the body with the ground, and the actual physiology of three dimensions, their two great subjects. We could call their vision 'down to earth'. But there is no one ethical or metaphysical temper, or vision of the future, that this version of materialism brings with it. The painter of the *Land of Cockaigne* is the painter of the *Triumph of Death*.

Bruegel is the monarch of down-to-earthness. One sign of that interest is the attention he pays to the human urge to make 'ground level' – make the earth even and measurable, patting it down and truing it up and mixing

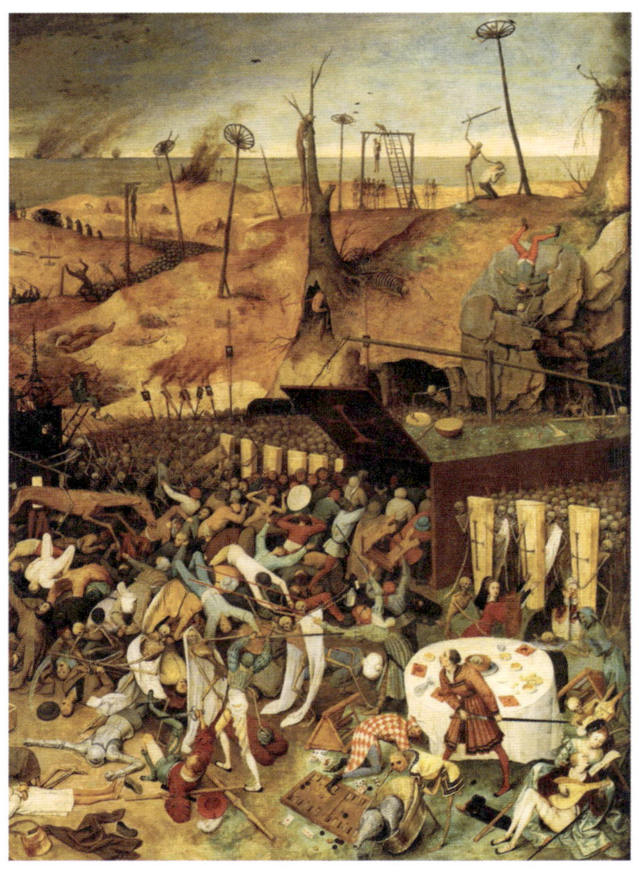

4. Pieter Bruegel the Elder,
The Triumph of Death, 1562–63, detail

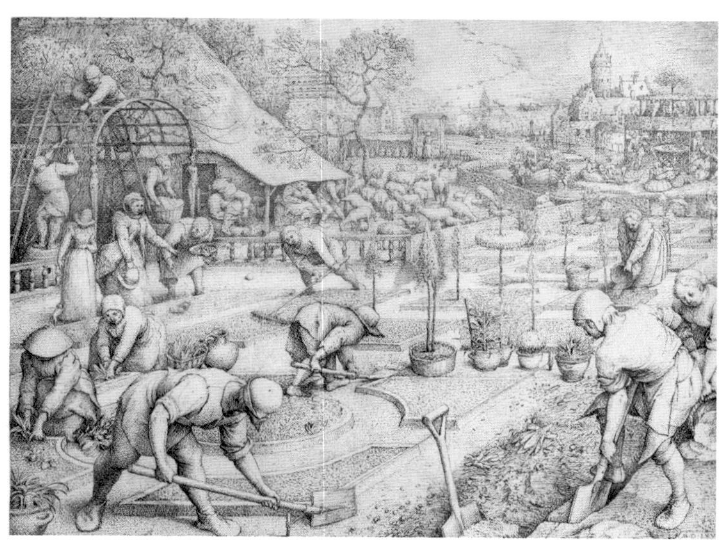

5. Pieter Bruegel the Elder,
Spring, 1565, pen and ink on paper

in drainage and mulch. It is typical – a further aspect of his materialism – that in the great drawing of *Spring*, done in 1565, Bruegel presents the activity as class-specific, and maybe a little silly.[5] The up-to-the-minute *parterre* in the drawing's foreground (the French word was beginning its travels through Europe at just this moment) chimes in with the young swells visible in the distance to the right, playing at nymphs and shepherds in a gazebo. There are signs of a humbler agriculture continuing – sheep shearers, a pigeon tower, a beehive on a hill, a man who looks to be hoeing – but they are crowded out by modern pastoral. A grand lady gives the gardener instructions. A floral barge pulls up beside the picnickers. The strict perspective of the flowerbeds participates in the gentle pedantry.

Ground level is a class achievement, but basic to the species. Edward Snow, in his wonderful book on Bruegel's *Children's Games*, puts this aspect of the painter's thinking in a nutshell. He homes in on a pair of figures far back in the *Children's Games* mêlée – a boy on stilts, and a little girl on the ground next to him, looking up, her face unsmiling, with arms thrown wide – and says this:

> Their juxtaposition is a key to the painting's
> anthropology. The human creature rises precariously
> on two feet (whose cumbersome black boots provide
> both immunity from the earth and anchored contact
> with it) and as a result has to devise for itself the world
> of functions and purposes which in nature seems
> merely given. One result is a paradox that the boy

on stilts neatly illustrates: the device by which he goes about acquiring a sense of balance and a feeling for the laws of the physical universe nurtures in him both a fantasy of transcendence and a preoccupation with downfall and ruin. It is difficult, in fact, to know which is host and which is parasite in this symbiosis.[6]

The fantasy of transcendence takes a different form in the *Land of Cockaigne*. What the man of letters at bottom right in *Cockaigne* seems to relish or aspire to is not so much teetering levitation as endless sluggishness or stasis. But even these terms have uprightness (or its opposite) built into them. *Stasis* in Greek originally meant 'standing'. The stadium was where well-adjusted bipedal bodies strove to remain upright while others fell down. The winners had their honed verticality immortalized in stone. Bruegel's imagining of stasis as roundness, repleteness and horizontality is charged, in other words – scandalous – at levels we barely recognize. Snow is right. A whole anthropology is in play.

There is one further thread to my understanding of Bruegel I ought to make clear at the start. For to talk thus affirmatively of Bruegel's 'whole anthropology', and invoke as positive a view of it as Snow's, is immediately to put myself on one side of a great divide in the Bruegel literature.[7] On the other stands that majority of scholars who seem convinced that the artist's account of the human condition is at best pessimistic and comically condescending, and at worst detached, moralistic, crisply repressive, coldly calculating in its provision (to a new

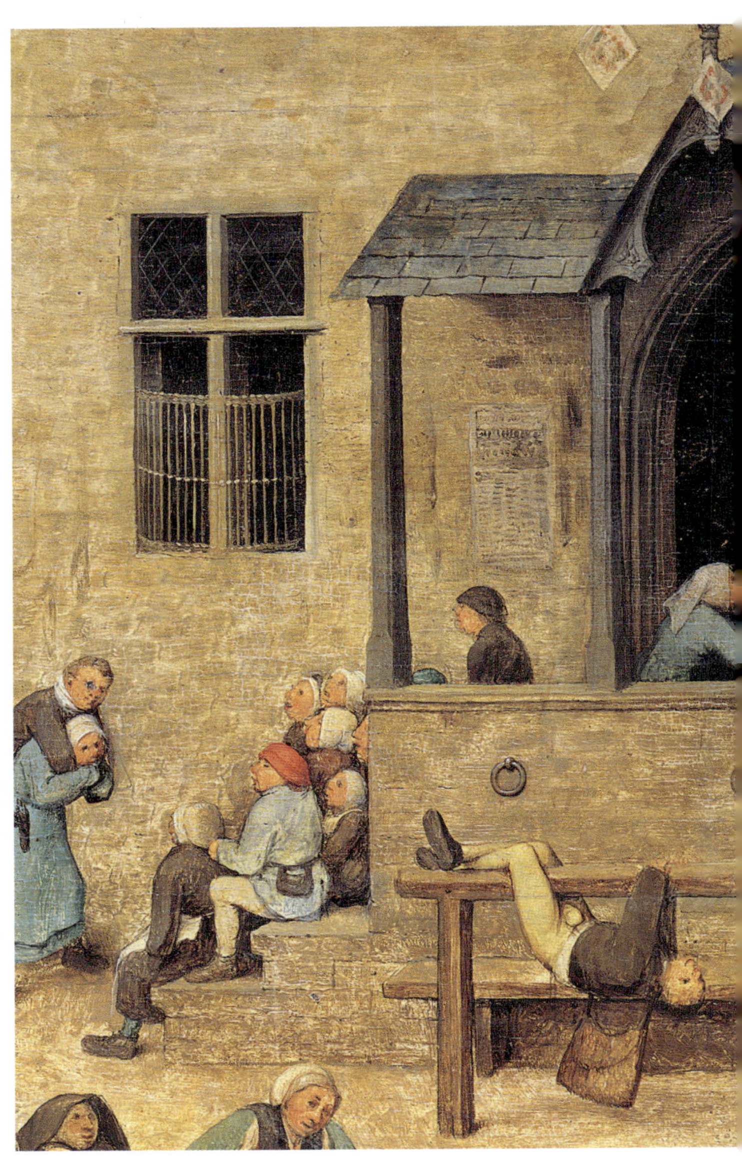

6. Pieter Bruegel the Elder,
Children's Games, 1560, detail

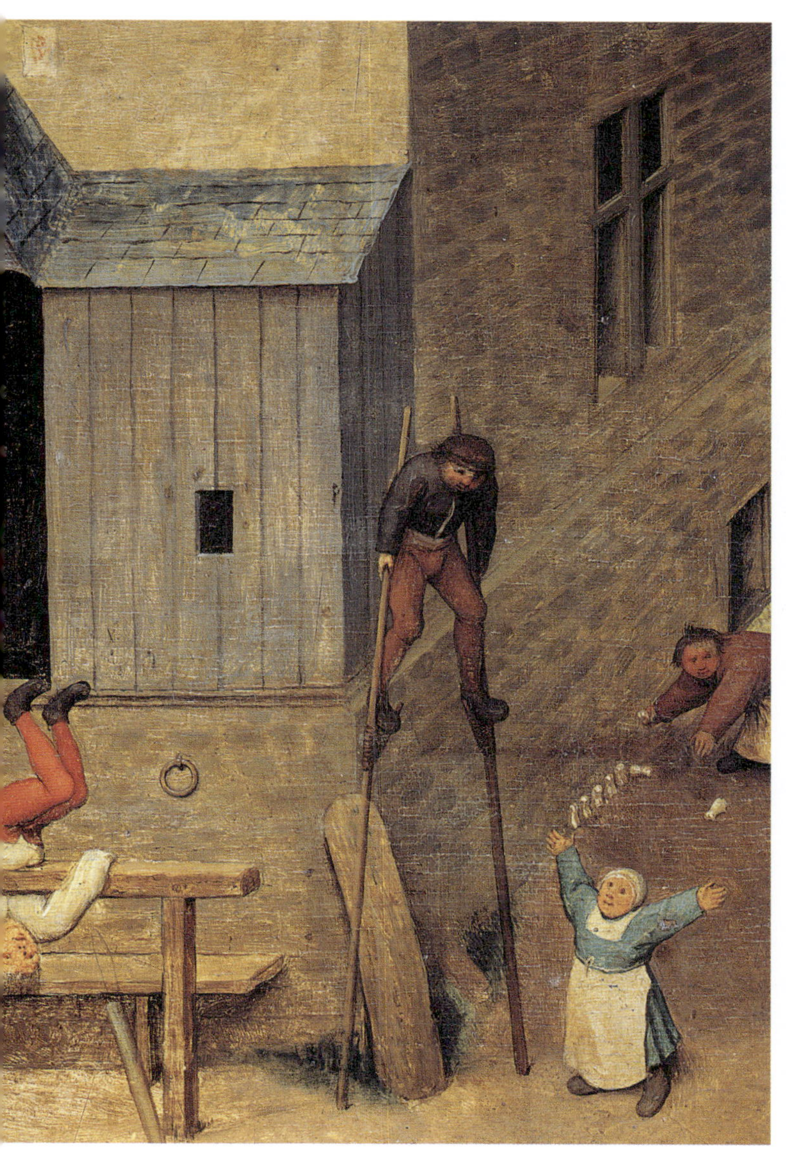

bourgeois audience) of the naive, the earthy, the old-fashioned and the grotesque.[8] This is the art historians' view of Bruegel, not the museum-goer's. It is, at last count, dominant among experts and, oddly, its strongest proponents have given it a distinctly ultra-Right or ultra-Left inflection. The voice that matters most here is that of the great Vienna formalist and enthusiastic Nazi party member Hans Sedlmayr. I quote the chilling climax of an essay on Bruegel he published in 1934:

> What could be the common denominator of the preferred motifs we have just identified – peasants, children, the deformed (cripples, the blind, epileptics, fools), the mass, apes, and madness? They are all manifestations of life in which the purely human borders on other, 'lower' states that threaten, dull, distort, or ape its substance. Primitives – a hollow form of the human; the mass – more raw and primitive than the individual man; the deformed – only half human; children – not yet completely human; the insane – no longer human. These are all liminal states of humanity in which and through which the nature of man is cast in doubt.[9]

Some of this resonates with the *Land of Cockaigne*. No doubt the particular choice of words in Sedlmayr's paragraph is telltale and repulsive. The slide from peasants to cripples, or masses to monkeys, wears its date and allegiance too much on its sleeve. But I am struck by the fact that so much of right-thinking, Left-leaning art history over the past decades has ended up assenting to a great deal of Sedlmayr's verdict – at least, on what Bruegel chose to show us of the human condition, and even why he did so.

I need to be careful. It would be scurrilous to quote directly any one of our recent hard-headed art historians in proximity to the 1934 text, and I do not for a moment wish to imply that behind their more up-to-date vision of Bruegel – Bruegel the cold ethnographic comedian, Bruegel the anatomist of lower-class folly, Bruegel the artist of modern bio-power – lurks a version of Sedlmayr's contempt for the non-normal. All I will say – and say it sharply, since the new 'progressive' certainty about art's essentially repressive mission and effect ought to be countered directly, with something of its own dismiss-iveness – is that Left and Right seem deeply to agree on the words that sum up Bruegel's attitude to his subject matter. His stance, for them, is of distance and conde-scension: achieved exteriority. The term that Sedlmayr brandishes is, predictably, *Entfremdung*, 'estrangement': meaning distortion, inexpressiveness, blank outwardness of appearance, human existence presented as a pano-ply of sluggish, intoxicated, absurd, degenerated mere behaviours. I do not see, in the actual descriptions many more recent art historians offer of Bruegel's treatment of his peasant actors, that in practice they dissent much from the *Entfremdung* diagnosis. And why should they, we might say, faced with the *Land of Cockaigne*? Does it not show us a world where even the hereafter 'borders on other, lower states'? Perhaps – but what follows from that proximity remains to be seen. Heaven may be shown to be earthly, even somnolent and ludicrous, without that being meant, *pace* Sedlmayr, to put the whole nature of man in doubt.

Let me begin with Bruegel's subject.[10] The basic idea of *Schlaraffenland* – a place where food is endlessly obtainable without effort, roast pigeon fly down obligingly into any mouth that has a hankering for them, houses are edible and fences made of a wicker of sausages – seems to have been a staple of the oral tradition in Europe long before it made its first textual appearances in the Middle Ages. The oldest written forms of the fable – a French *fabliau* from the middle of the thirteenth century, probably written in Picardy, or *The Land of Cokaygne*, a slightly later poem in English – already look to be turning the 'folk' material to purposes that are hard to grasp.[11] They may even be parodies of heaven. Who they were written by, and for, and against, are questions that exercise scholars. But one dimension to the legend was basic to its appeal: it posited a world in which abundance overflows class distinction. And this side of the story loomed large after 1450: in its language and cast of characters, *Schlaraffenland* became more and more explicitly 'popular'.[12] (As usual in such cases, this does not mean that its appeal was restricted to the lower classes. The doings of peasants and proletarians, real or imaginary, seem to have amused and horrified their betters.) In the sixteenth century, alongside repeated textual retellings, *Schlaraffenland* began to be the subject of woodblocks and engravings.

Mostly the prints were perfunctorily drawn – perhaps naivety was part of the point. We have, for example, a fluent but rudimentary woodblock *Das gelobte abgebildete Schlaraffen-Land*, done by a German workshop in the second half of the century, which is fully 2 feet high and over 3 feet wide, put together from eight separate blocks.[13] It is a kind of alternative world map or *Triumph of Greed*. Bruegel stays close to many of the standard features of such depictions: notice the woodblock's great mountain range made of buckwheat porridge, through which hopefuls have to eat their way to the promised land (with one prominent new arrival spewing and farting as a result), or the fence of sausages and house of tarts, or the pig with the knife holstered in its side – for which, in the print, a second newcomer reaches before the porridge has fully disgorged him.

Naturally, some of the written forms taken by the legend in the 1500s pulled it into higher ideological space. It was moralized, often sententiously; its tall tales of another world were updated, lightly, perhaps with a view to poking fun at the vogue for travellers' tales following (and preceding) 1492; there is even a moment or two in the texts – Herman Pleij has pointed them out – where the narrator seems to be toying with the notion that *Schlaraffenland* is connected to contemporary heresies.[14] Two manuscript poems in Middle Dutch – one of them dating from the first decade of the sixteenth century, but both recording much older material – put the kingdom, in passing, under the sign of the Holy Spirit. 'Dit is 't lant van den Heilgen Gheest.' Or again, more forcefully, 'Dat land maeckden

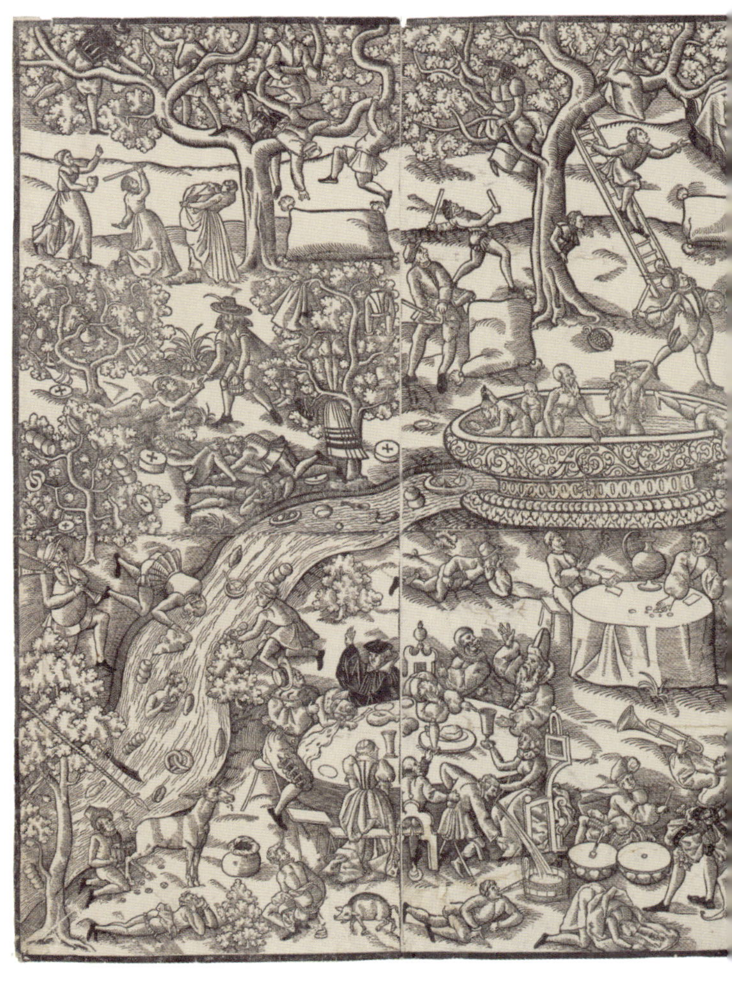

7. Anon, *Das gelobte abgebildete Schlaraffen-Land*, *c.* 1500–99, woodcut

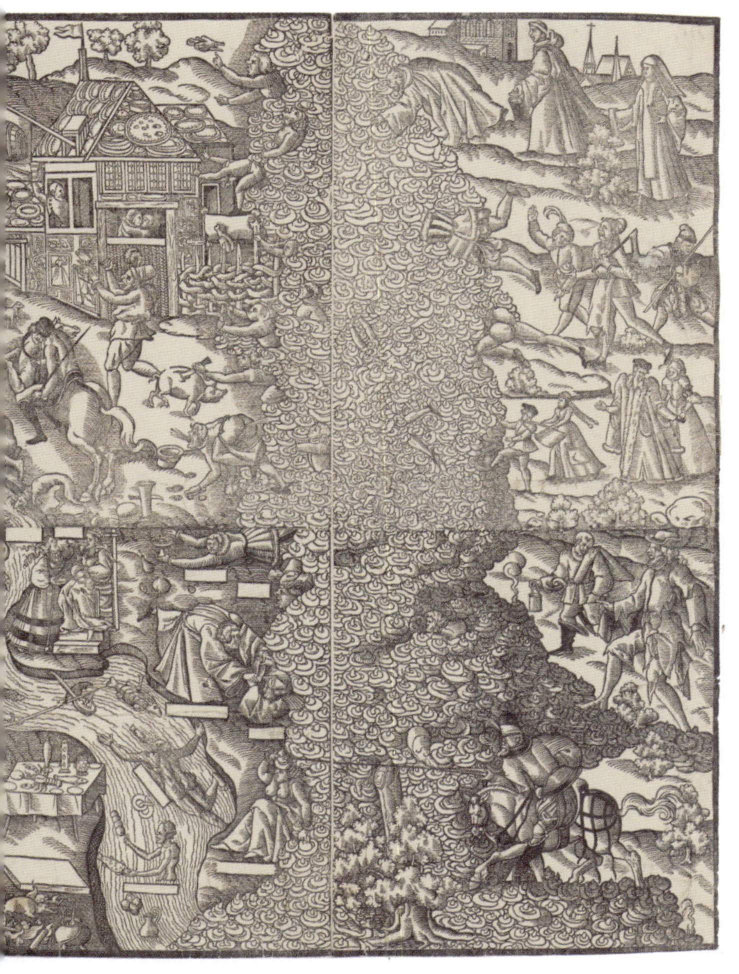

dye Heylige Geist.' The jibe is outlandish, and in a time of Reformation potentially blasphemous: it makes no sense unless as a facetious reference to Adamite and 'Brethren of the Free Spirit' invocations of the Holy Ghost – accompanied as they were by dreams of (and experiments in) a new age of erotic godliness – which we know were on authorities' minds.

Cockaigne was a magnet: the legend's imagining of abundance attracted to it all kinds of new and old material. But the modernizings and moralizings do not touch the heart of the matter or explain the legend's continuing appeal. *Schlaraffenland* was not, after all, primarily a realm of Free Spirit eroticism: its genius was gluttony, not lust. Nor did the prints and poems insist on parallels with Brazil or Hispaniola: the costumes and flora of the giant woodcut are typical in being so firmly Northern European. A poem of 1546 may end by reminding the reader of the link between *Luye-leckerlandt* and criminality – 'Until now this land was known to no one except Do-nothings [*Deugh-nieten*], who were its first discoverers, and it is to be found next to the gallows'[15] – and many of the chapbooks are similarly stern. But the basic light-heartedness of *Schlaraffenland* shrugs off these messages from the pulpit.

It seems clear from the woodblocks' image repertoire (the textual material sometimes suggests as much) that Cockaigne was originally connected to carnival in the popular imagination – to the battle between Carnival and Lent – and spoke to the enduring peasant economy of feast and famine.[16] Whether or not it is true that dearth and malnourishment actually increased in the late Middle Ages – the statistics are fragmentary, and a general answer is anyway beside the point – Pleij and others marshal a body of evidence to suggest that the *fear* of hunger grew from 1450 on, and with it the habit of publicly eating to excess.[17] Urban spectacles were incomplete without floats piled high with food, and a final wild stuffing and swilling by the crowd. The performance has the look of a defence mechanism – a 'ritual surfeit designed to banish all thoughts of scarcity'. The world of Bruegel's *Fat Kitchen* and *Big Fish Eat Little Fish* is close.

In the *Land of Cockaigne* hunger is a thing of the past. That is the ruling counterfactual. No doubt certain viewers of Bruegel's painting – and buyers of the engraving made of it, perhaps after Bruegel's death – would have been capable of making the connection with the New World. Maybe one or two even caught a whiff of the Free Spirit. But what Bruegel drew on most deeply were the dreams and wishes – and the sense of those wishes' ordinary unfulfilment – that had made the story worth telling for centuries.

'Bruegel's heaven is an empty place,' wrote Max Friedländer. 'Only the earth, the here and now, was his proper realm.'[18] 'For Bruegel man was quite definitely not created in the image of God.'[19] 'The world looked to him like a kind of clockwork that never needed winding.'[20] The last remark in particular comes back to mind each time I confront *Cockaigne* again and feel its world turning slowly – vertiginously – on the axle of the tree trunk. All of Friedländer's judgments strike home. They

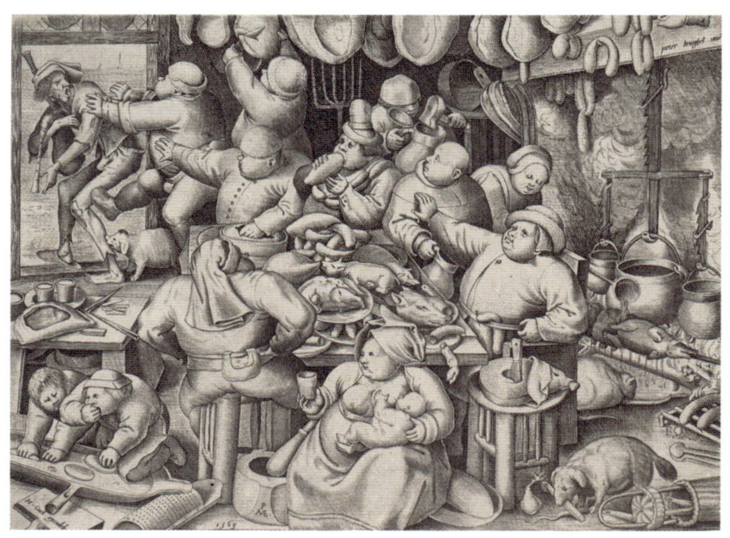

8. Pieter van der Heyden, after Pieter Bruegel
the Elder, *Fat Kitchen*, 1563, engraving

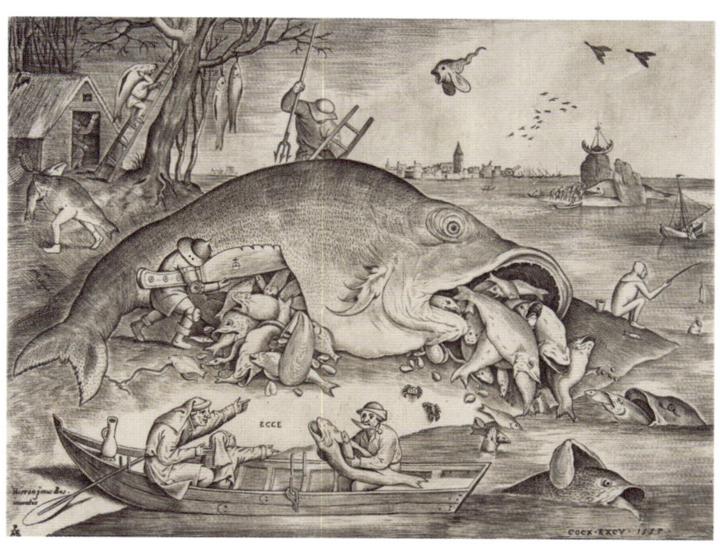

9. Pieter van der Heyden, after Pieter Bruegel
the Elder, *Big Fish Eat Little Fish*, 1557, engraving

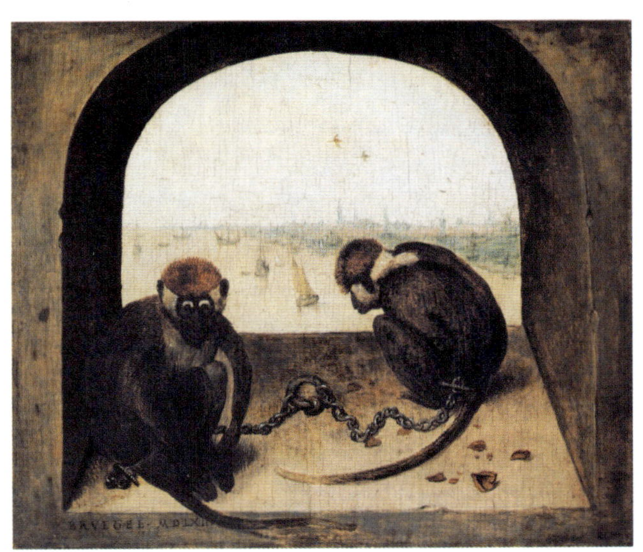

10. Pieter Bruegel the Elder,
Two Monkeys, 1562

help us with the *Dark Day* and *The Cripples*, I feel – and even with the terrible *Two Monkeys* – in ways that more careful contextualizations cannot.

But they may go too far. One guesses that Friedländer, looking at *Cockaigne*, would not for a moment have taken its 'alternative world' gambit seriously, or thought Bruegel and his audience did. The verdict he passes on the emptiness of Bruegel's heaven is followed, in the same sentence, by essentially the same verdict on the painter's hell: it 'is populated almost exclusively by Boschian creatures'. In other words, hell for Bruegel (says Friedländer) is essentially a second-hand concept – a leftover, a tissue of quotations – only imaginable through the medium of a previous genius. And whatever (still mysterious) specific orthodoxy or heterodoxy may have provided Bosch's vision in the first place with its motive power and perhaps some of its motifs, by the time Bruegel was addressing it the vision was a relic of the previous century.[21] Bosch had become the 'Boschian'. The visionary had declined to the grotesque.

Whether we think of *Cockaigne* as heavenly or hellish – or in the end neither – it is remarkable, among the thirty or so paintings from Bruegel's last four years, for being the only one to imagine (on the other side of the mountain) an alternative reality. And it is quietly, relentlessly anti-Boschian in so doing. The hybrid and the multiform have no place here. A fence of sausages and a cactus of loaves are assemblages, not mutations. The non-world is made from wholly (banally) worldly materials. Improbable things may be happening in the hereafter, but identities are not threatened. Eternity is in love with the productions of time. But does this mean that Friedländer is right, that for this artist 'the earth, the here and now' are all there is?

Believe it or not, the art-historical consensus regarding Bruegel's intentions in *Cockaigne* is that he did it as a warning against gluttony.[22] I shall dispense with the battery of quotations, but I am hardly sharpening or simplifying their basic message: the purpose of the painting, say the authorities, was to show gorging and idleness for the sins they are.

This seems to me on a par with saying that Jane Austen's *Sense and Sensibility* is all about how sense is preferable to sensibility as a guide to conduct. Well yes, that appears to be the book's premise, and roughly its conclusion, but it is not what makes the book interesting – it is not what structures the play of Austen's attention and makes generations of readers wish to pick up its thread. I dare say Bruegel believed that overeating was a bad thing: one has no quarrel with the printmaker's assistant who thought that words to that effect ought to go at the bottom of the *Cockaigne* engraving ('Those lazy and greedy peasants, soldiers, and clerks / arrive there and sample everything without having to work'[23]); but it seems to me an improbable, absurd hypothesis that Bruegel painted the picture in the first place – *this* picture, the picture painted this way – to illustrate the truism. *Cockaigne* is a study in ontology, not ethics. It is out to make us see and feel things, not remember what we are supposed to think about them.

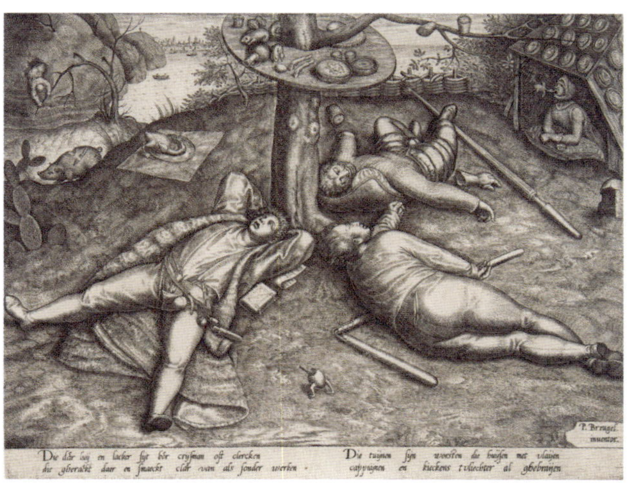

11. Pieter van der Heyden, attrib, after Pieter Bruegel
the Elder, *Land of Cockaigne*, after 1570, engraving

The *Cockaigne* panel is not big. It measures, to repeat, just over 20 inches by just short of 31: barely half the width of its savage pendant, done a year later, *The Blind Leading the Blind*. Size, in Bruegel, does not correlate with ambition. His *Sea Battle off Naples* had compressed the scene of history into 16 inches by 27, and revelled in what miniaturization – the strange bird's-eye view of the sea and Vesuvius – could do to its objects. His *Cripples* fill a panel measuring 7¼ inches by 8½ inches, the size seemingly intended to force us to look closely when we would rather not. But there is a sense in which the dimensions and shape of *Cockaigne* are even more unsettling – because it is harder to put one's finger immediately on where the format means to situate us in relation to the objects portrayed – and sometimes in the literature it is suggested that the panel has been cut down. On the basis of the engraving it must have lost no more than an inch at the top, unless the damage was done before the engraver got a look. In any case the print is unreliable. It slices an inch or so from the edge of the painting abutting the lean-to of tarts (notice what happens to the standing cheese in the print, and the hinge of the roof as it meets the picture corner), so who is to know if it did not add as well as subtract? The printmaker is struggling with something fundamental in the Bruegel and well beyond his pictorial capacities.

He struggles with proximity and interruption. There is a feeling in *Cockaigne* of things being close, the tree and its tabletop sleeve just as much as the egg and the sole of the young clerk's shoe; and of everything tipping

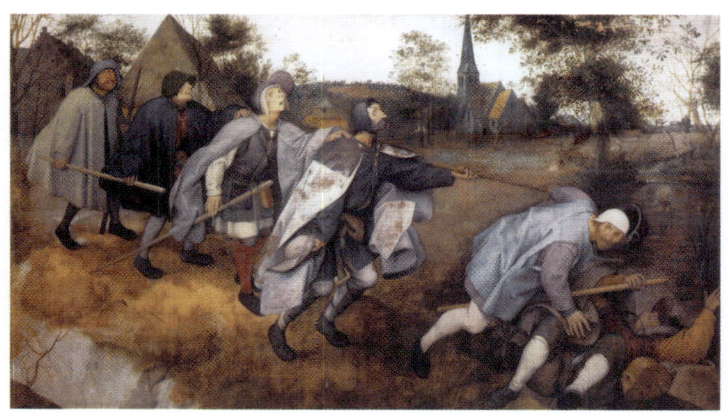

12. Pieter Bruegel the Elder, *The Blind Leading the Blind*, 1568, tempera on canvas

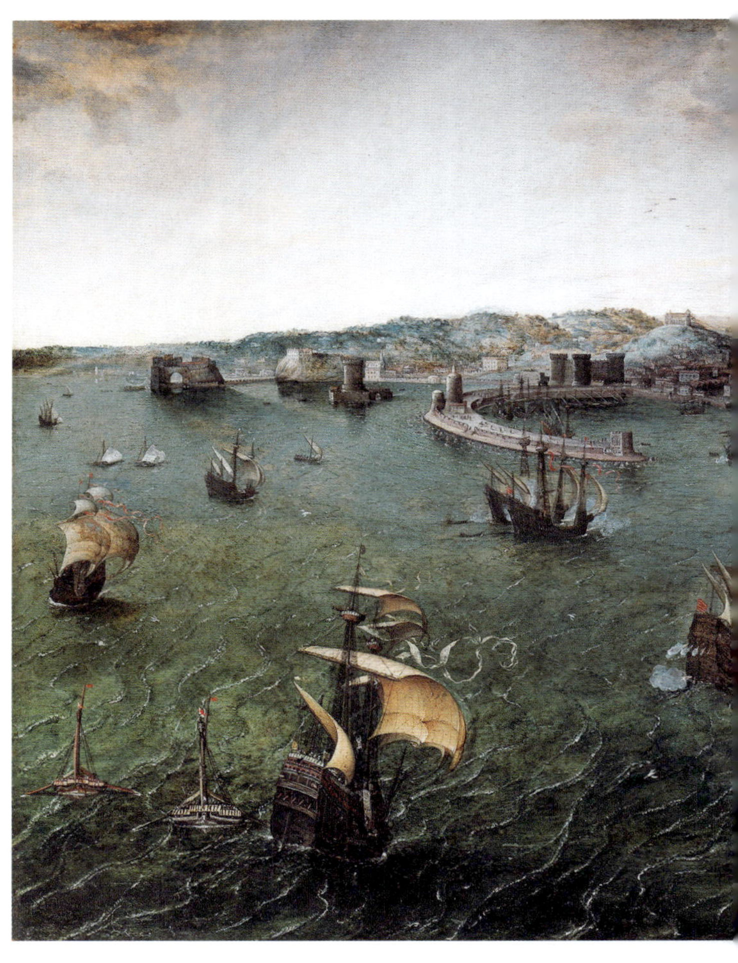

13. Pieter Bruegel the Elder,
Sea Battle off Naples, 1563

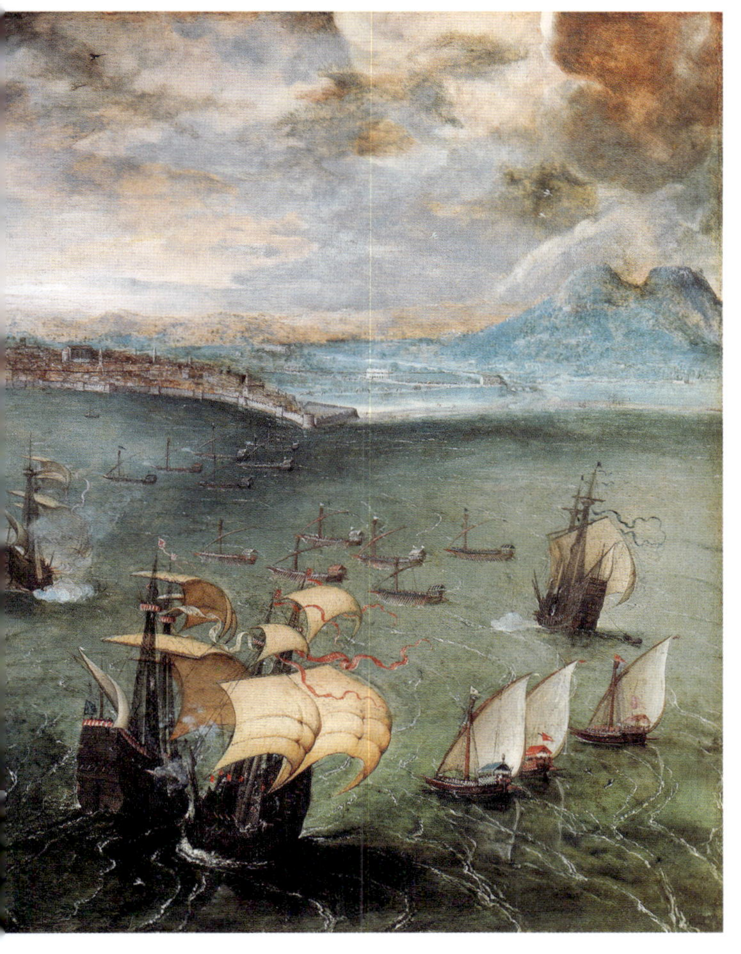

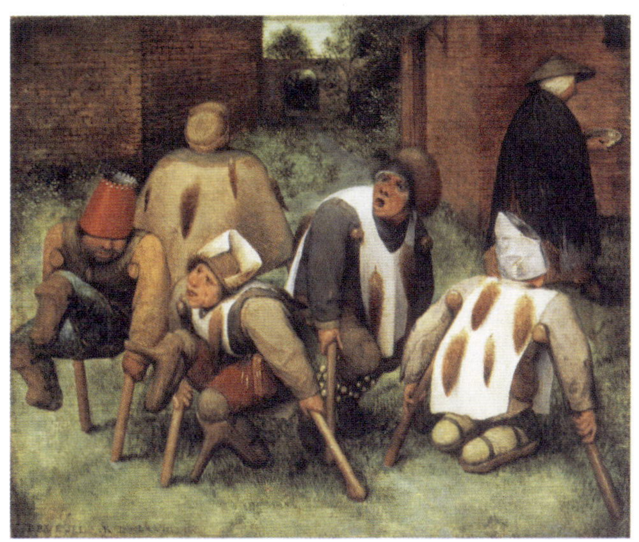

14. Pieter Bruegel the Elder,
The Cripples, 1568

and tilting towards the viewer, so that the egg has to work hard to keep its balance on the foreground slope. There is a feeling of things being crossed arbitrarily by the edge of the visual field: not just the trunk, branch and table, but the cactus of loaves to the right, and above all the lean-to with the tarts. The top left corner of the panel takes a slice out of the lean-to's architecture the way a knife takes a slice out of the cheese; and the slice delights in having us guess, and give up, at the general logic of the structure it cuts into. It echoes the painting as a whole in this. Corners are wonderful in *Cockaigne* – the roof, the buckwheat mountain at top right, the grass giving way to a chasm below – but they only confirm the general impression of stumbling into a space that never was. The porridge rolls into the picture like a lava flow.

Compare *Cockaigne* with what most scholars now agree was its closest visual source, an engraving by Peeter Baltens done maybe six or seven years earlier.[24] We know Bruegel and Baltens were acquainted and worked together at the start of the 1550s on an altarpiece for a glovers' guild; and there is no doubt that Bruegel took over his basic rough structure from Baltens's print, as well as one or two visual jokes – even the idea of a piece of tableware falling from the tree, suspended for ever on its way to the peasant's thick head. Baltens's image is fumbling and fussy, but in comparison with the Bruegel at least it *tries* to apply the new laws of perspective. In the event, the older artist makes a hash of them and cannot get his sprawling figures sorted out properly across a receding ground plane. But he knows what he is supposed to do: he struggles to keep his horizon

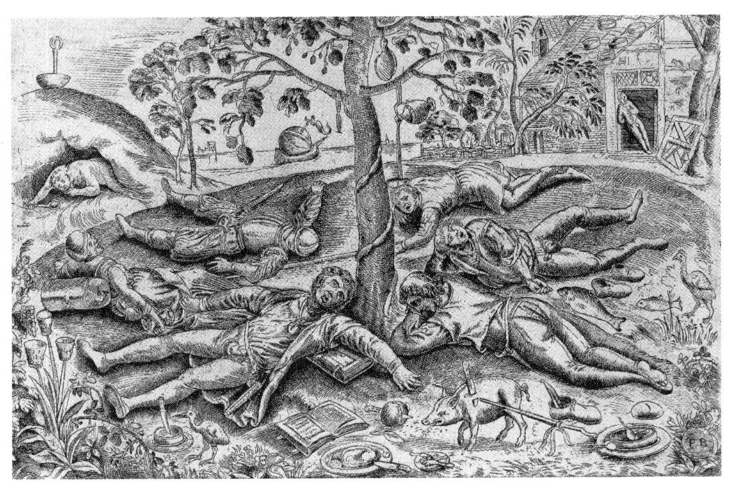

15. Peeter Baltens, *Land of Cockaigne*,
1560s, detail, engraving

line low (in the modern way) and have his house of tarts, top right, be plausibly rectangular. There is even a door off its hinges in front of it, like a perspective drawing frame. Bruegel, by contrast, deliberately closes and fills up and pushes everything towards the picture plane. The line of the hill grows higher; the house becomes a half-folded tent; the buckwheat mountain adheres to its corner; the tree sprouts its unplaceable tabletop; the egg spells out the gradient up front. Spatially, the whole panel is more like a frame from the journeyman's eight-block *Schlaraffenland* than the Baltens Bruegel had in front of him.

What Bruegel does here to Baltens's space is typical of his painting during the last four years of his life. It is as if he became confident, after making the anchored and intricate spaces of his 'Months of the Year' series in 1565, that from now on he could work – he needed to work – with two kinds of perspective in a picture at once. He would return to the map-like, broadsheet spread of spaces characteristic of his earlier *Children's Games* or the *Procession to Calvary* or *Carnival and Lent*, but now have that kind of disposition interact with a space felt as empty, palpable, proximate. Not that 'perspective' had been lacking in the previous pictures – think only of the endless street in *Children's Games* – but it had tended to cede to something like a bird's-eye view as things got larger and closer. In *Cockaigne*, by contrast, the space conjured up by the rim of the table does not peter out at some point adjacent to the picture plane, giving way to the surface world of the egg: it somehow *includes* that surface world, looming over it, lending it geometry. (Block out the

tabletop with one hand, even in front of a reproduction, and the foreground is robbed of half its vitality.)
Perspective and broadsheet are in balance. The tree to
the right, in front of the buckwheat mountain, is pure
silhouette but also, one comes to realize, a bending,
extruding entity in space – grabbed by the indefatigable
mountaineer, and sucked in by the glacier of porridge.

Bruegel's *Cockaigne* is not crowded. The picture is
one of the most striking examples of Bruegel's habit late
in life of reversing a theme that seemed naturally to call
for abundance and multiplication of episodes, in the way
of the prints and texts, and instead restricting it, reducing
it to a particular closed space and focused cast of characters.[25] It is typical of the older Bruegel that he should
individualize the idea of excess. Of course the individuals
in *Cockaigne* are carefully chosen and stand for the separate orders of society as Bruegel's world understood them
– much more clearly than in Baltens, say.[26] Peasant with
flail; cleric with book; soldier with lance and armoured
glove; and a further man in armour vegetating under the
roof of tarts – by the look of him maybe a full-blown knight
to the other one's mercenary, though one cannot be sure.
(It is important that military men predominate. The year,
to say it again, is 1567: the Duke of Alba is massing his
troops. It would have been foolhardy of Bruegel to risk
too direct a comment on the subject, but some scholars
believe that the soldier on the ground is wearing specifically Spanish uniform and even sporting a Spanish
moustache.[27]) All the figures are fascinating, that is, but
surely the most spellbinding of them, around whose

wide-open eyes the whole picture seems to orbit, is the young man to the right lying on his folded fur coat. Let us call him the 'man of letters' – one of the *clercken,* as the caption on the engraving has it. The clerk's inkpots and penholder are still laced delicately to his belt, part of an array of ties and strings that seems to be barely holding together under the pressure of his swollen stomach. He may be specifically a clergyman – the book beside him has the look of a Bible – but he could as well be a notary or wandering scribe. The manuscript being crushed by his sleeve has a legal look. He is brother to the man with the pens cavorting in the foreground of the Bruegel *Wedding Dance* now in Detroit.

I shall speak to the point of this cast of characters eventually, but first let me focus on there being so few of them. What does the reduction make possible? Certainly a stress on the main bodies' weight and shape – the bursting seams, the slipping codpiece. But this is bound up with an emptying – or at least a relative clearing – of the ground plane up front, which means that the substance and surface texture of the grass, and above all the grass's orientation, become subjects in themselves. Relatively little is happening on Bruegel's hillside, and therefore its richness and strangeness and uncertainty of incline – its tipping and wheeling, as if in sympathetic response to the wild disc of the tree-table – attract our attention. That we can see the sole of the man of letters' shoe only makes the question of where we stand in relation to the earth it rests on the more puzzling. But surfaces here, whatever their orientation, are transfixing. The grass is

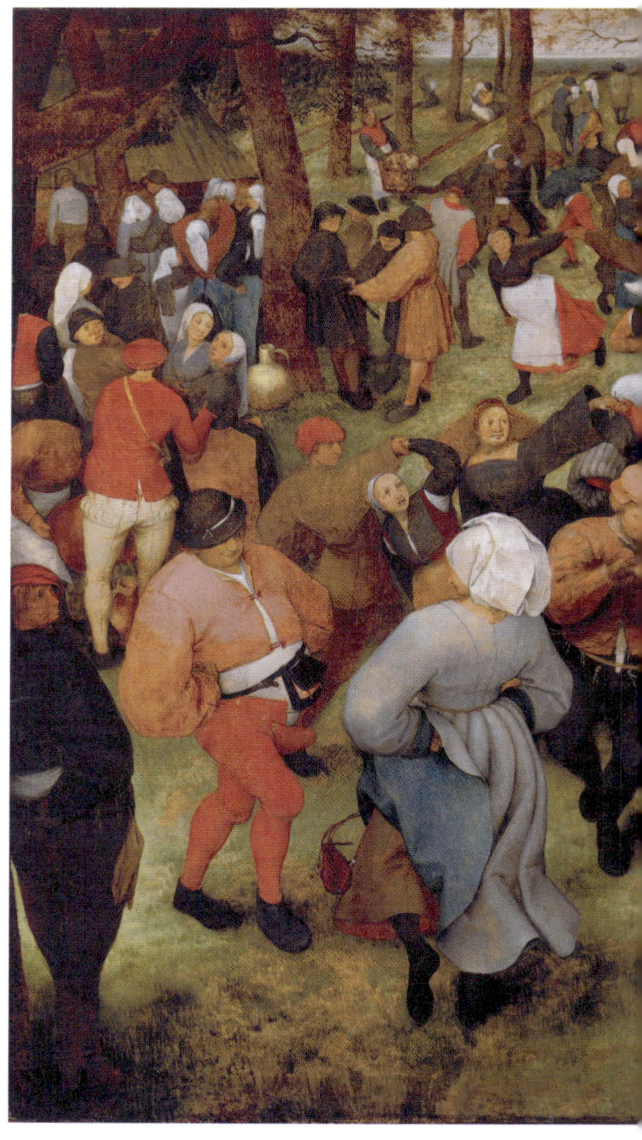

16. Pieter Bruegel the Elder, *Wedding Dance*, 1566

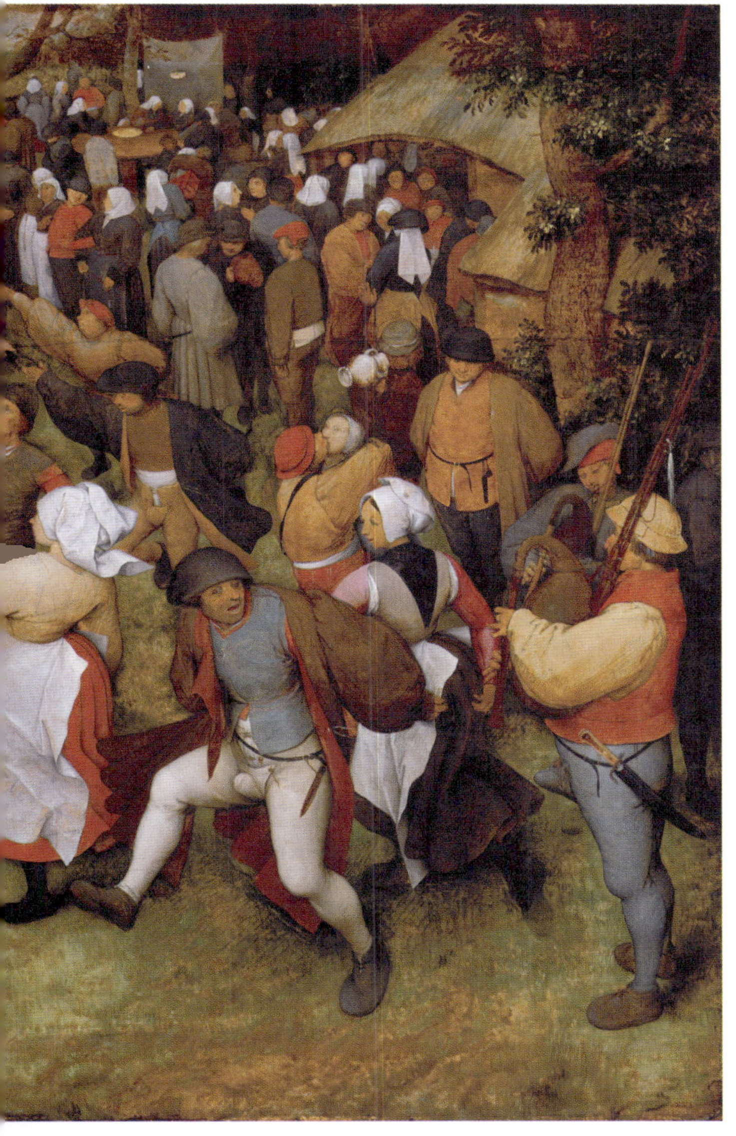

a marbled, aqueous green, every square inch fretted and patted by the painter's brush. The fur is a slightly cruder rehearsal of the same procedure, as if to alert us to the softness and variance of the grass; the mercenary's chain mail is the variation mechanized. Of course the earth is infected by the analogy with fat asses and plumped-up pillows. It is a swelling belly, as smooth and elastic as the mountain of gruel. The sausage fence just spells out its slippery rotundity. Yet none of this is stressed or improbable. The earth is round, the globe turns slowly on its axis. The tree is an axle, with the bodies spokes to its wheel. The great shape of the ground plane does no more than confirm the new science.

Tilting in *Cockaigne*, then – and tilting and distending seem to be the picture's two topological models – carries a special, equivocal ethical charge. It is disorienting, but not overmuch. Most things stay put on the canting table. The scene is unstable, but not utterly shifting and precipitous. The swell is that of a pillow, not a wave. (The sea is flat calm and sunlit.) Tipping and swelling seem to coexist quite happily with this world's naive delight in geometry. The fastidious square of the tablecloth on the grass; the ellipse of the table, and those of the cactus plant; the house of tarts; the zigzag of lance and flail; the neat segments cut from the cheese and pig; the fowl's touching eagerness to fit the parameters of its pewter dish. It is true the hillside lacks horizontals, and in large part verticals to match. The tree is a poor substitute for an upright body – especially *this* tree, collared and truncated, halfway between living thing and piece of furniture. But I do not see the absence of flats and uprights as morally (ontologically) improper, a sign of the human world degenerating. Regressing, yes – but sometimes that means becoming more itself. The Book of Common Prayer says simply 'that by reason of the frailty of our nature we cannot always stand upright'.[28] *Cockaigne*'s tone has the same forbearance.

Clothes are important here. It is telltale that Bruegel's Garden of Earthly Delights has no place for nakedness. (Or for sex in general. It is a male world, only partly demilitarized.) Friedländer says that Bruegel's difference from his Italian contemporaries hinges essentially on his lack of interest in clothing as 'drapery' – that is, as a system of folds whose purpose is to reveal the logic of the organism underneath.[29] The northerner's painting moves in the opposite direction. What it aims for is the outline – the whole shape of a body or an entity, and the kind of energy or inertia the shape conveys. Bruegel's world is a compilation of unique particulars, not a structure built out of ultimately abstract – infinitely interchangeable – gradients of tone and colour. Clothes are a source of endless fascination for him, exactly because they combine with bodies in such unpredictable ways – sometimes revealing and articulating them, sometimes concealing and muffling. He never stops cataloguing the ludicrous intricacy of apparel. The ties and knots and over-elaborateness all round the man of letters' midriff in *Cockaigne*, for example, are answered by the steady calligraphy on the soldier's trousers – contour lines all leading to Mount Codpiece. Bruegel especially delights in clothing that seems to be taking on a life of its own, maybe in the process robbing what it clothes of life. The iron glove still feels for the lance. The codpiece was the artist's preferred piece of human flummery (as the ruff was Rembrandt's or the wimple Van der Weyden's) just because it was extraneous, and what it claimed to be covering might or might not be there in anything like the form that the covering implied. All clothing is armour or prosthesis. Human beings are not bodies in Bruegel, even when they have eaten their fill and lie there like over-enlargements of themselves: they are outfits with bodies in hiding.

There is not a lot going on in the *Land of Cockaigne*, and Friedländer is again right that this marks the picture off from Bruegel's world in general, which is usually pullulating with activity. Even when the cast of characters is restricted, the main actors are usually frantically on the move. The very idea of 'world' for the artist is summed up, in his *Misanthrope* from 1568, by a goggle-eyed cutpurse pushing against the glass globe he has to live in, driven – driven mad – by wants, needs, schemes, delight in wrongdoing. In *Cockaigne*, by contrast, the clockwork has run down – but not stopped. The fur cloak of the man of letters transmutes matter-of-factly into the grass next door. Everything here is still capable of becoming something else, but not dramatically, not in some moment of metamorphosis. There is no hurry in *Cockaigne*. The pig is ambling, the egg is a child taking its first steps. Engulfing seems to be a better metaphor for change than metamorphosis – like the sticky grey hillside swallowing the tree. Change is digestion.

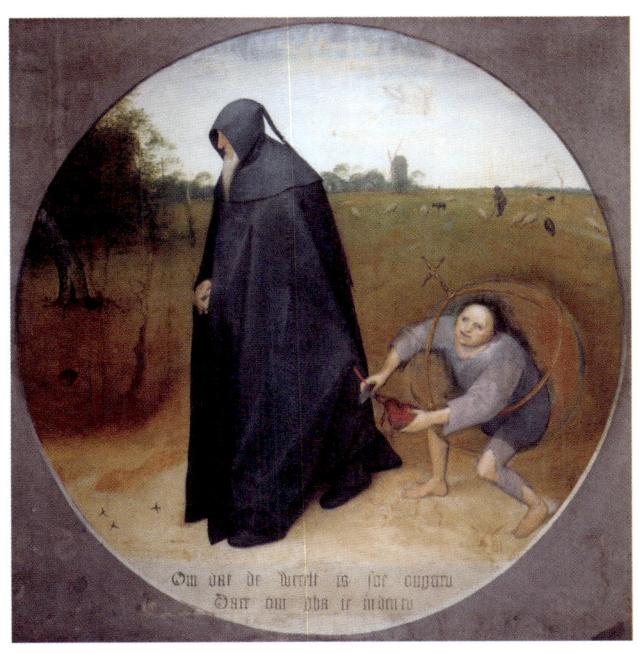

17. Pieter Bruegel the Elder, *The Misanthrope*,
1568, tempera on canvas

What would a world be like – this looks to be Bruegel's question – in which all human activities slowed to the pace of the large intestine? Thought, too: the man of letters is still visibly cogitating, but in the way of the woman in Bruegel's earlier *Netherlandish Proverbs*, who stares from her window at a stork flying past. Or compare him with the gooseherd in *Proverbs*, pondering the bipedalism of his charges: 'Hierom en daarom gaan de ganzen barrevoets', 'For one reason or another geese walk barefoot'. I for one do not believe that Bruegel, in seizing on this peasant recognition (part ironical, part acquiescent) of the way the world goes on presenting us with too many things to think about, wanted us to disapprove of blank wonder – of endless staring into space.[30] He had done some staring in his time.

Excretion is naturally part of things in *Cockaigne*. The man with the spoon falls into paradise like a turd from an anus. We know that shitting was something Bruegel habitually painted with affection and seems to have meant as a sign of life going on regardless. Shitting at the foot of the gallows (in the picture now at Darmstadt) is not so much cocking a snook at the Law as putting the world of culture in perspective and showing us what of nature will never say die. Shitting at the base of the Tower of Babel (in the picture in Vienna) has a similar valence. It takes place in a meadow where working people are taking a break between *corvées*. Some are swimming. One man is washing his smalls in the stream. The unobtrusive activities (the figures are tiny) go with the friendly lie of the land. The shitting figure is far away, but deliberately close on the picture surface to the emperor up front paying a visit to his folly, with stonemasons grovelling at his feet.[31]

Maybe the people in Bruegel's paradise still exist in the shadow of death. Surfeit is close to insensibility. No one here looks immortal. The young cleric seems to have his eyes fixed on something ominous, or at least a puzzle. Darkness surrounds him. I can imagine a reading of the *Land of Cockaigne*, it follows, that would start from the resemblance between its overloaded tree-table and that of the feckless courtiers in the *Triumph of Death*, ignoring (or trying to resist) the skeleton army. But such a reading would miss Bruegel's tone. The egg is not an actor in a morality play.

So what kind of play is it in?

An answer should start again from the source material – the basic mode of *Schlaraffenland*, and what we can guess about the mode's appeal. No one *believed* in the land of Cockaigne. It was a comic thought experiment: not a vision, not a utopia (it did not posit itself as perfection nor as perfection gone wrong), not even really a wish-fulfilment. Wish-fulfilments do not spell out their absurdity as they proceed.

Cockaigne seems originally to have been a product of the oral culture of the European peasantry; and the legend's fundamental ludicrousness, its unfathomable cynicism and materialism – including its cynicism *about* materialism, at least in utopian guise (its resistance to the move from imagining to positing) – tell us something

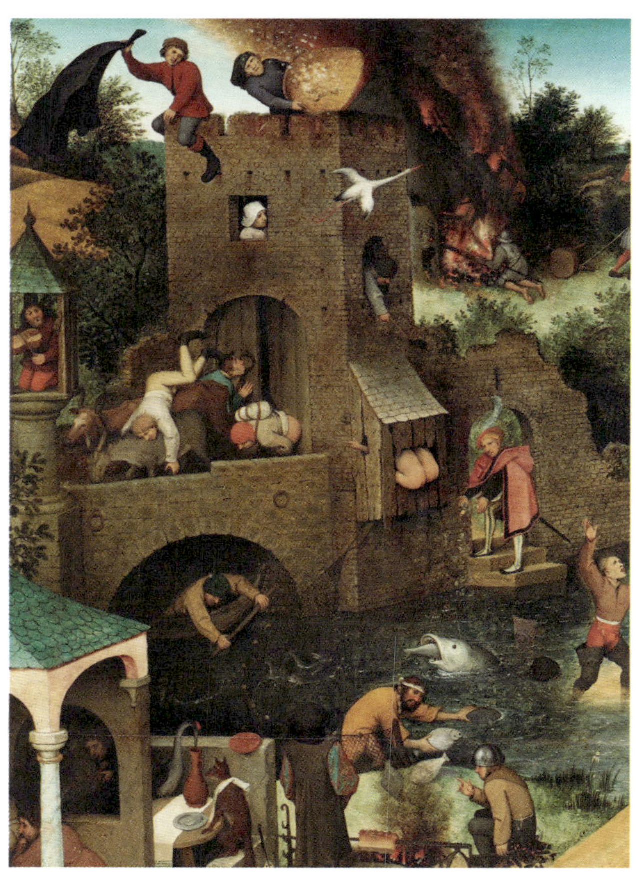

18. Pieter Bruegel the Elder,
Netherlandish Proverbs, 1559, detail

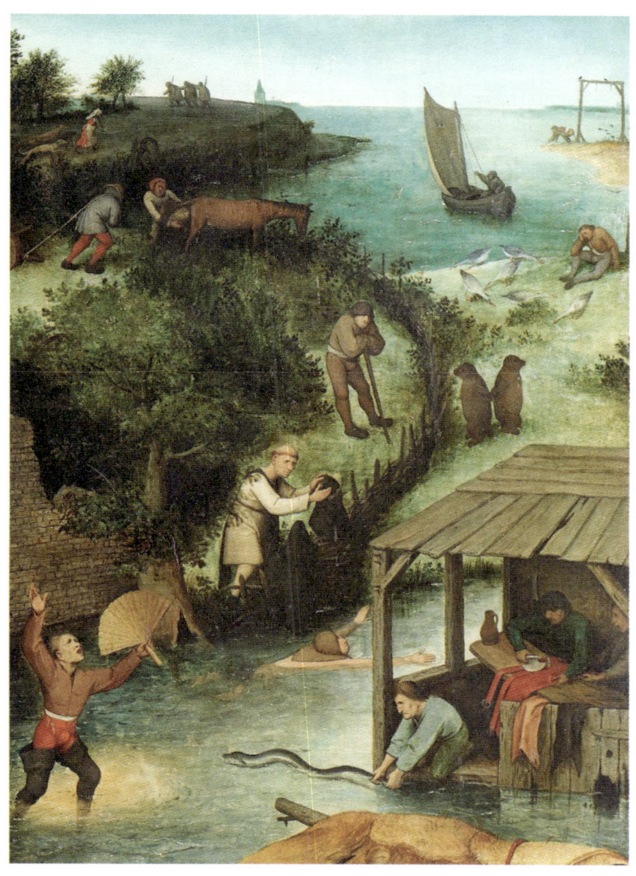

19. Pieter Bruegel the Elder,
Netherlandish Proverbs, 1559, detail

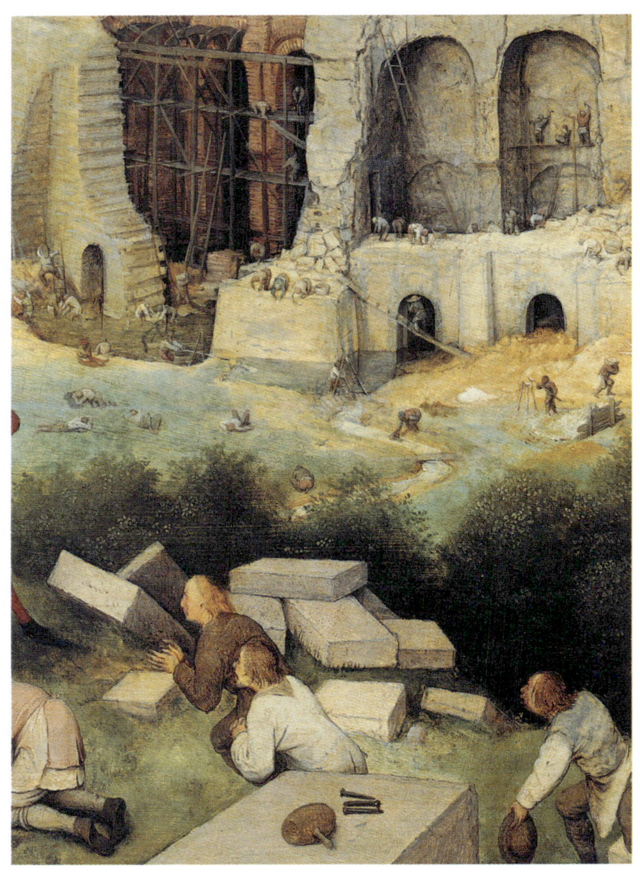

20. Pieter Bruegel the Elder,
Tower of Babel, 1563, detail

central about the texture of that vanished culture, of which we shall never know much.

Bruegel's painting responds deeply to *Schlaraffenland*'s spirit. It is make-believe, not utopia; and its controlled unseriousness is what allows it to think so deeply and humanely about what the material world consists of, what the human animal is in its simple physical existence, what being fully and exclusively in the material world could be like. The unseriousness of the ethical and epistemological frame is what makes the ontology possible. Obviously Bruegel was aware of how closely the bodies and objects of his counterfactual world duplicated – inflated, hypertrophied, but also in some sense perfected and realized – those of his factual one. Laughing at exhaustion and satiety was a way of discovering more fully what both are, physically, experientially, gravitationally.

Cockaigne is a picture of gravity – of the pull of a gravitational field, of pleasure as a planetary system with cooked food as its sun. *Cockaigne* celebrates the cooked as opposed to the raw, we could say; or, rather, the cooked replacing the raw altogether. It is a place where the founding distinction of Lévi-Strauss's or Detienne's 'civilization' has been permanently left behind.[32] The last unconscious residues of the palaeolithic have vanished from the cultural bloodstream. No more sacrifice and butchery; no more blood (the lance is discarded); no more shadow of the cross.

And yet ... isn't Bruegel the artist who reminds us most constantly, following Genesis, that 'In the sweat of thy face shalt thou eat bread, till thou return unto the ground; for out of it wast thou taken'?[33] Compare *Cockaigne* with the

Harvest. We surely would not need to know which picture of ease from one's labours came first – the man of letters under the table or the mower in the *Harvest* resting against the tree trunk – to sense that, for Bruegel, the two states were inseparable. One was always conceived as a variant of the other. (Still, in *Cockaigne*, the peasant lies uncomfortably on top of his flail. And his eyes are open – maybe more in exhaustion than satiety.) In fact, chronologically, the mower in *Harvest* preceded the clerk. Bruegel, that is, dreams the impossible in terms of the everyday; but also – always – in terms of the everyday world's extremity, of the way the everyday never ceases producing the horrible, the preposterous, the luxuriant, the eternal. Eternity here (remembering Friedländer) means nothing more than the mad wish for stasis – for final fulfilment and perfection – that is constantly present in workaday life, haunting it, taking advantage of it, making it bearable. Bruegel, in short, is the opposite of a utopian; but this exactly does not mean that he reverses utopia's terms, or is even straightforwardly a pessimist. For no one has ever had such an eye as he did for the non-existent in what exists, for everything in human affairs that pushes insatiably towards non-identity: the will to pleasure as much as the will to power, playfulness as much as vacancy, the bride in the *Peasant Wedding* – dwelling for ever and ever in the moment – as much as the cripples' frantic determination to move on. The *Dark Day* is his vision of the good life.

It is typical of Bruegel that his vision of things transfigured, when at last he allows himself one, should not be The World Upside Down. The hereafter in *Cockaigne* is the world as it would be if it became more fully itself, with its basic structures unaltered and above all its physicality, its orientation, intact. The World The Same Way Up, Only More So.

We come to the question of Bruegel and Christianity.

Consider the *Triumph of Death* in Madrid.[34] How common a subject was it in Bruegel's time? And where does the title come from? No doubt the basic idea stems from the world of late-medieval prints and wall painting: one of the last times I saw the picture it resonated immediately with a great Dance of Death, done around 1500, encountered a few weeks before in Burgundy, at the parish church of La Ferté-Loupière. That image-world was Bruegel's inheritance. But this surely meant he was all the more aware that, in turning a Dance of Death into a panorama of Death's Final Solution – a disciplined army carrying out a scorched earth policy – he was steering away from the Dooms he could see in the churches towards something more down-to-earth and terrible. The *Triumph* is Hell, and also Last Judgment, but now with the dead coming out of their graves not to accept reward or punishment, but simply to take revenge on the living. Discreetly but unmistakably, Bruegel insists on the closeness of the story he is telling to that of Christian resurrection of the body. Twice he shows members of the skeleton crew busily digging up the coffins of their comrades, and right at the centre of the painting, in the distance, is a skeleton stepping from his grave. Not far away stands a horrible,

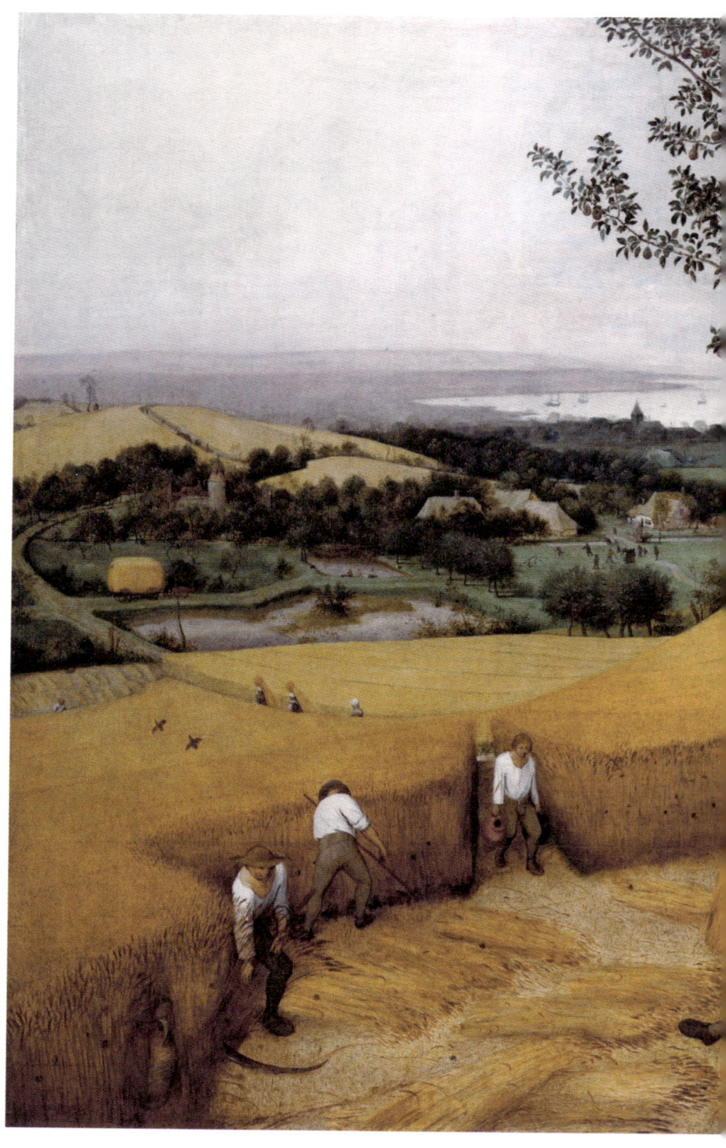

21. Pieter Bruegel the Elder, *Harvest*, 1565

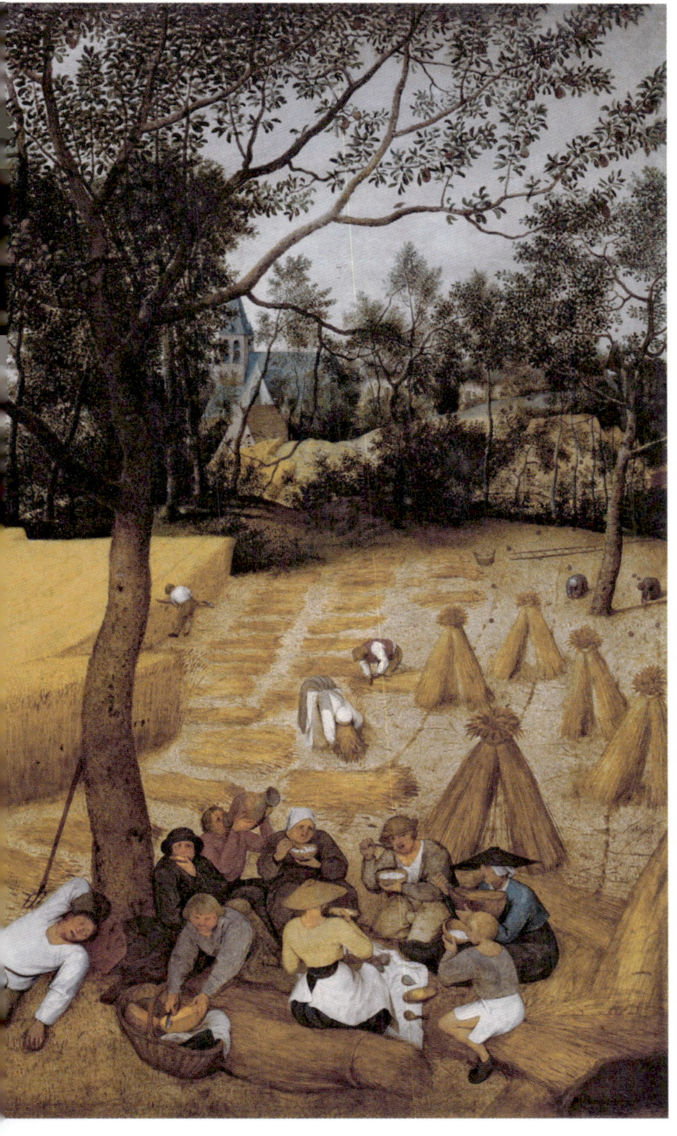

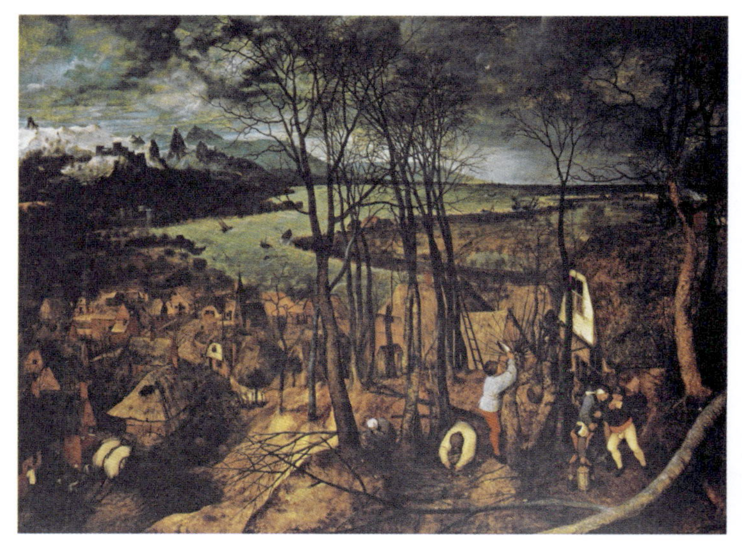

22. Pieter Bruegel the Elder,
Dark Day, 1565

blood-red filigree cross: signs of Christian burial are swallowed in the general tide of malignancy.

The skeletons are human. They are excited, eager, well-drilled, mechanical, patient, vindictive, cheaply satirical (especially when faced with courtly love) and occasionally despairing, tired of the monotonous one-sided game. At the stern of a ship of death to the left is a skeleton sitting disconsolately with one heel on the ice. Here, if anywhere, may be the limit case of Bruegel's pessimism. Even the work of death becomes boring, and one or two killers fall out of line. What's the use, even of mortality?

It is not quite right to call Death's soldiers skeletons. Some have desiccated flesh still clinging to their ribs. And it looks as if they see the enemy as not merely the living, but also the too recently dead – the too fleshy, with too much of this world still about them. Otherwise what is the point of their dragging off corpses lying at rest in open coffins, as seems to be happening centre foreground? Why does the skeleton closest to us bother to slit the throat of an unresisting character already wearing a shroud? Death does not like clothes, perhaps: he does not like any kind of bodily envelope, natural or artificial. He will enforce the bare minimum.

Hell is an afterthought in the *Triumph of Death*, almost as if it were a concession to Boschian taste. Torture takes too much time. Demons appear round the edges of a black castle-kiosk stage centre, but they and their building look flimsy, like a carnival float. Perhaps the coffin-tunnel over to the right in the picture is the entrance to

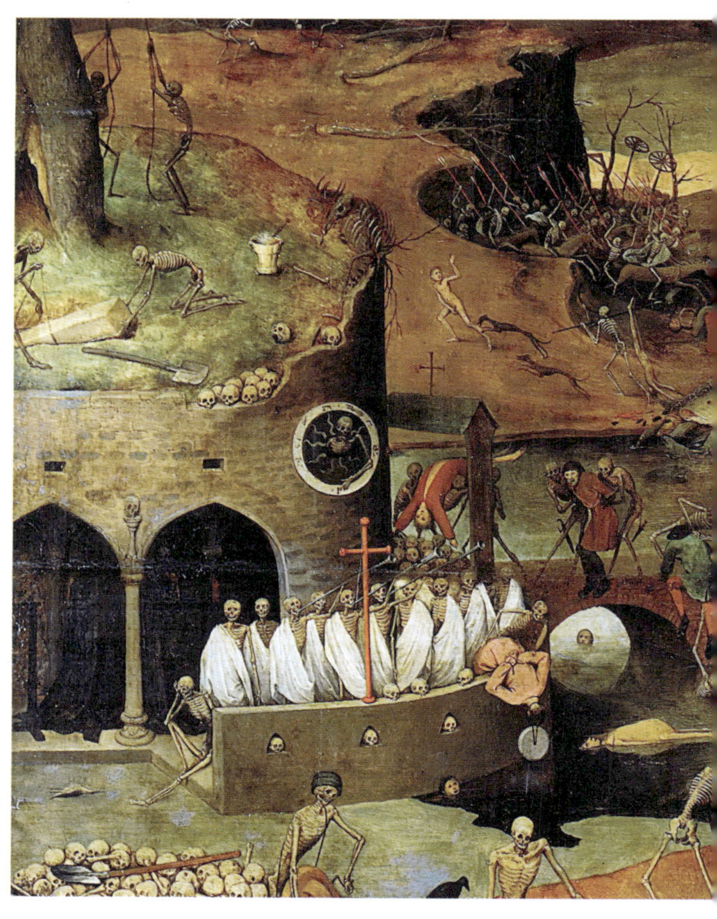

23. Pieter Bruegel the Elder,
The Triumph of Death, 1562–63, detail

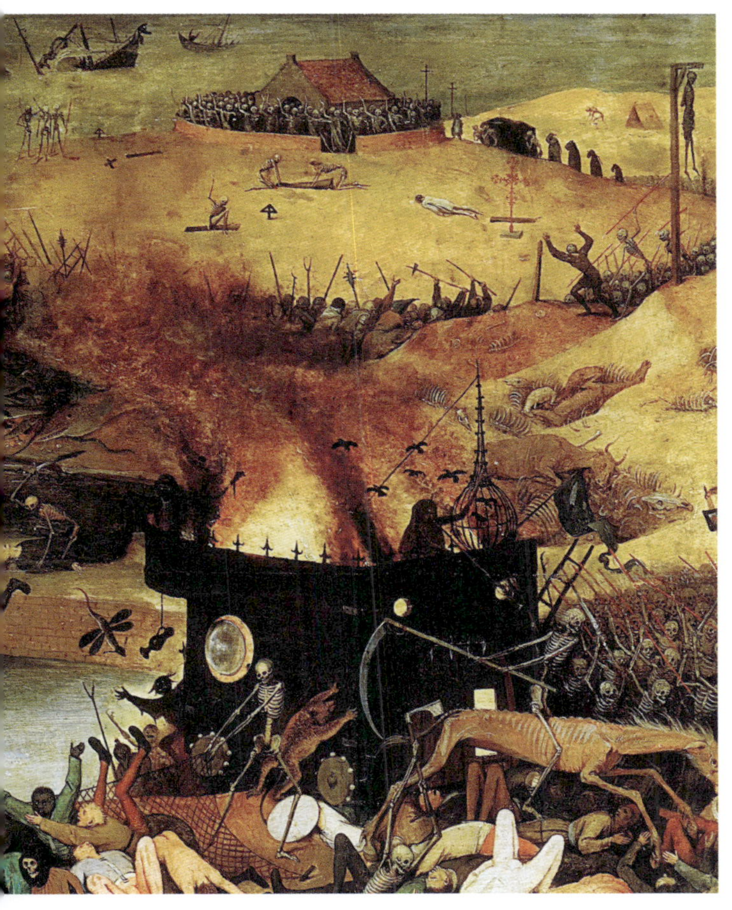

an underworld (though its floor seems level), but there is nothing to indicate where the darkness inside is leading. The structure resembles a holding pen. The living stream into it as if of their own free will, thinking it a way out, or at least a change. Death as we see it is done familiarly, with knives and swords. Skeletons are ordinary executioners. The hills are provided with a few more gibbets than usual. Smoke and fire on the horizon do not seem to promise a plunge into a Bosch-type pit: they just indicate – the signs would have been commonplace – that war is everywhere.

Two Deaths in the distance are busily felling trees. (Photosynthesis is uncongenial to them. Brown and yellow are their colours.) A skeleton sprouts from a clock face on a building, its bony finger pointing at 1. A naked man is chased by starving dogs and tries to shield his privates with one hand. Is it modesty, or an awareness that this is where the dogs will start? What will the skeletons do with the splintered and scattered bones in evidence at the foot of the gibbets? Reassemble them? Or are some deaths – those administered routinely on earth, long before Death's army arrived – too total for even Death to reanimate?

What Bruegel does to the image of hell in *Triumph* – that is, the ruthlessness with which he eliminates hell's distance, hell's otherworldliness – may help us with what he does in *Cockaigne* to the image of heaven.[35] The question, again, is why the *Schlaraffenland* story appealed to its audience and why it survived in early modernity. The answer may be this: Cockaigne was a dream world, but also repeatedly in the telling a parody of dream worlds.

This meant that the legend could be brightly topical in the world following 1492, where marvels and alternatives were the talk of the town. But the story was not simply up to date: it spoke to something deeper in Europe's consciousness than travellers' tales or the wilder shores of Anabaptism. Cockaigne – the core idea, the basic counterfactual – was a parody of paradise. It was a desublimation of the idea of heaven: an un-Divine Comedy, which fully made sense only in relation to all the other (ordinary, instituted) offers of otherworldliness circulating in late medieval culture. What it most deeply made fun of was the religious impulse, or one main form the impulse took: the wish for escape from mortal existence, the dream of immortality, the idea of transcendence itself. 'And God shall wipe away all tears from their eyes; and there shall be no more death, neither sorrow, nor crying, neither shall there be any more pain: for the former things are passed away.' What Cockaigne said back to religion – and here its voice seems that of peasant culture itself, in one of its ineradicable modes – was that all visions of escape and perfectibility are haunted by the worldly realities they pretend to transfigure. (Blake's 'Proverb of Hell' on the subject, which I have quoted more than once, does no more than put in a nutshell the 'materialist' wisdom underlying the un-hellish proverbs Bruegel grew up with.) Every Eden is the earth intensified; immortality is mortality continuing; every vision of bliss is bodily and appetitive through and through. Cockaigne speaks back especially to the Christian world of mortification – all the more unanswerably for refusing to occupy the same moral high ground, and shrugging off the spiritual with a smile. To all of this – the deep structure of the legend, so to speak, and the reason for its persistence – Bruegel's picture answers profoundly.

But the legend, to repeat, is *unserious* – not despairing or sardonic or even *anti*-utopian, exactly. And don't those adjectives apply to Bruegel's retelling? Isn't the atmosphere of his *Cockaigne* decisively heavier and grimmer than that of the Baltens print, or the eight-block *Schlaraffenland*, or anything in the chapbooks? Aren't the horrors of 1567 in the background?

Some have thought so: Friedländer, for instance. I know there are viewers in front of *Cockaigne* who are struck by the painting's brownness and barrenness, and recoil from its vision of stunned immobility.[36] Paradise is just death dressed up, they reckon. The pseudo-animation of the bones and egg on the tabletop, doing their skeleton tapdance: that is the key to this afterlife.

There will never, of course, be a satisfactory answer to the question of Bruegel's pessimism – to the depth of resignation or despair built into his humour. He lived in merciless times. Certainly it is hard to see much sign of God's grace in the world he shows us. His view of humanity certainly includes – insists on, time and again – the species' capacity for cruelty and gullibility. World-weariness and world-revulsion (vanity of vanities) were clearly familiar to him, as to his culture as a whole. But I do not think, finally, that the bones dancing on the table sum up the painting's temper. There is no crisp or irrefutable way of saying why not: in a case as com-plex as Bruegel's, issuing from a world where complex thinking had to state its conclusions guardedly, it will always be a matter of intuitions, responses to atmosphere, understandings of placement, the weight given to certain details, the vertigo (or euphoria) brought on by painting's stopping of everything in its tracks.

Paradise, so the great visionaries tell us, will possess a light of its own. The light in *Cockaigne* is a characteristic Bruegel achievement. When one sees the panel in the small room it occupies in Munich – I remember a January day, with grey sky reflecting snow – it is often brighter and paler than in memory or reproduction. Time of day and height of the sun are hard to interpret. The wonderful white glare on the sea could be that of an endless wind-less afternoon. There is an amount of darkness, though never deep shadow, in the picture's middle ground, under the table and up towards the fence of sausages. Perhaps brown is the panel's predominant colour, though the soft grass green of the foreground – which hits home first as the picture comes in view, and only slowly stops drowning out the pinks, reds, yellows, whites and greys – is worked into and over the brown across fully two-thirds of the picture surface.

Sometimes when the atmospherics are good in Munich it seems as if the effect Bruegel must have wanted was a variant on the one he perfected in the *Harvest* (in many ways *Cockaigne*'s closest point of reference): the same ivory haze on the edge of thickening into overcast. That would make sense of the light on the sea. Is there even a faint sun in the sky over the distant city? But the comparison with *Harvest* soon breaks down. *Cockaigne* is darker: not dismally dark – I resist the idea of the dream world as barren or ominous – but in the end not quite partaking of any daylight or half-light we can recognize.

The green is astonishing: no one analogy will lay hold of it. It does have a wonderful watery lightness, like marble or a throw of extra-fine velvet, but it is not in the least stony or marble-smooth or aqueous. It is grassy, obviously, maybe even mossy, but dry; like a thin, almost papery covering on top of the earth; in places (towards front right, for example) it seems like the colouring of a rock face.

The falling away of the green into a chasm is unmistakable when one is in front of the real thing in Munich – far more so than in any reproduction. At bottom left, especially, grass gives way to earth. But again, whatever upset and instability the tilt of the land may bring on is more than counteracted – this is my answer to the idea of *Cockaigne* as the world in negative – by the painting's relish for things, details, textures, contours, all the contents of the world's full stomach.

There is no good way of repeating the relish in words. Pointing out and enumerating are what language is designed to do, whereas what is glorious in *Cockaigne* is just pointless endless proliferation. Look at the airholes in the cheese! Look at the excellent ironwork on the flail. Or the fine silver clamps on the Bible. How exquisite the man of letters' face – pink cheeks and nose, glinting eyes, delicate nostrils and lips. Look at the flayed-flesh pink of his tunic and leggings, the latter like exposed tissue.

Compare the furred lightness of the soldier's chainmail. How beautiful the drawing of the young man's shirt, especially its neckline and long liquid folds. Notice the roots of the tree by the mountain of gruel – a typical Bruegel interest here in the character of a particular root system, plus a specific kind of spreading into the surrounding earth, and a set of outrider saplings.

Two of the cactus loaves are half sunk in the grass, like tombstones. The peasant has a thick mane of hair. The soldier's lance is steel-tipped, glinting even in the shadow. The egg in the foreground has yolk spilling down the right side of its shell!

Some of these wonders must have been worked on meticulously and at length. But Bruegel is entirely a 'modern' painter, and much of the panel's surface was evidently covered fast, the freehand movement of the pigment throwing up and half cancelling identities. All round the foot of the cactus of loaves, for instance, there are thrown-off commas and curlicues of brown that would not look out of place in a Corot. At the bottom edge of the tablecloth, just to the left, the signs of speed are unmistakable: grass comes up the line of the white cloth, smudging over it at one point, retreating from it at others, with the panel's primed ground still visible. Side by side, the grass and the man of letters' fur lining alert the viewer to the handmade character of both. In the same way that the little bush's blotted, transparent leaves against the sea (just to the right of the tabletop) make the viscosity and stodginess of the porridge opposite more palpable.

None of the dictionaries agree with me, but I cannot help thinking that the homophony between the word 'Cockaigne' and the useful substance extracted from the coca plant is not coincidental. I imagine a nineteenth-century pharmacologist, naming and sampling, getting at least a brief laugh from the way the new anaesthetic chimed in with the old. And this licenses me to say a word or two about the difference between Bruegel's dream of consumption – his vision of pleasure and fulfilment – and ours. The relation of heaven to appetite is always a question: the schoolmen worried about angels' intestinal tracts.[37]

Bruegel lived at the moment just before 'consumer society', which is to say, before the world of goods accelerated and expanded in the first age of globalization, before the mass production of commodities, and before the notion of bodily well-being was transformed by a 'modern' multiplication of addictive substances compatible with the new tempo and discipline of production.[38] The idea of consumption in Bruegel had surfeit as its ruling figure – eating and drinking to the point where wild dancing breaks out, or men and women fall helplessly to the ground. Consuming for Bruegel (and his culture, by the look of it) meant primarily ingesting, relishing, dreaming a full identity with the world of things, swallowing them whole. He would not have understood, I think – or rather, would not have had much sympathy for – the world to come, with its carefully regulated doses of pleasure, its quarter-intoxications, its small hits and highs: caffeine, tobacco, cane sugar, the international alcohols (rum, gin and so forth), opium and its derivatives, and, later, the pharmutopia of anxiety and despair.

Consumption went on for Bruegel's contemporaries under the sign of scarcity and insecurity. *Cockaigne* is not heavy with soldiers for nothing. It was a dream of the opposite to a world of toil and malnutrition: a still world, a fat world, an idle and irresponsible world, a world of bodies. And none of these descriptions apply to the dream of consumption that now possesses us. An intensification of 'consumption' is not only compatible lately with an increase in the pace of work and in hours spent on the job – we surely do not need statistics to convince us that the past forty years in the West have seen an extraordinary speed-up and hyper-exploitation of white-collar labour – it is a condition of that increase. Consuming and recreation go on at the pace of work, in work's shrinking interstices, using an apparatus that has to present itself as an extension of – a magnification and perfection of – the gadgets and disciplines we come home from. The gym is a factory; the big game an animated spreadsheet; the body sweating on the treadmill is turned away as decisively from its actual carnal experiences – towards the TV on the wall, or the calorie app on the iPhone – as the coldest Weberian Puritan balancing his ethical and financial books.

Bruegel's world of consumption was oriented to the notion of anti-work. Therefore play was one of its basic categories: that is why in talking so eloquently about *Children's Games* Edward Snow could give us a view of Bruegel as a whole. But play only fulfils its human potential – only carries an insubordinate charge – if it is posited as counterweight to the grown-up world of purposiveness. We, on the other hand, exist in a world where the 'adult' and the 'juvenile' are hopelessly commingled; where leisure time has been both increasingly infantilized and increasingly regulated, domesticated, depoliticized, dosed and packaged. The infantilized and the commodified are one. Bruegel's terms are different. He goes in for the childish, the foolish, the grotesque and the boorish, as opposed to the infantile – which last is a word that really gathers force only in the eighteenth century, and does not spawn the verbal form 'infantilize' till the twentieth. Consumer society for Bruegel was still bound up with the festive, the gargantuan, the multitudinous, the carnivalesque: all the kinds of performative community, in other words, that preceded the great clean-up we call 'modern'. Whether Bruegel approved of the performances does not concern me. How modern he was is an unanswerable question.[39] He showed us the non-modern bodies in action; he inhabited and articulated them. That is what counts.

We go back to the ground in *Cockaigne*, and Bruegel's treatment of standing and falling.

Bruegel – to put it briefly – was a connoisseur of bipedalism. Edward Snow is right: humankind's posture determines Bruegel's view of the species. By the time he does the pen drawing called the *Fall of the Magician Hermogenes*, probably in 1564, the artist's view of the impossible and demonic in existence – of the non-human, that is – has clarified to the point of pedagogy. The banner in the magician's room spells out the argument in picture language: to diverge from the human, which is what Hermogenes' disciples are bent on achieving, is to do something else than stand on two legs. Magic is upside-downness, or levitation, or walking the tightrope, or standing on one's hands; or, ultimately, having a body in which the 'up' of ingestion, perception and production of language and the 'down' of standing firm, moving forward, excreting and copulating are utterly scrambled. The creature in the foreground of *Hermogenes* balancing the bowl on its groin sums this up.

One comic consequence of this loss of bearings, Bruegel likes to point out, is what happens to the phallus. Both of the humanoids on the banner – one of them crablike on all fours, the other crawling on his belly with legs flapping as decorative appendages (like coxcombs) – are given the last touch of monstrosity by their codpieces' being extruded from their bodies by the logic of their poses, inviting an opponent's knife. (Codpieces, we know, were regularly a focus of Bruegel's attention. Part of that, too, was bound up with his anthropology – for codpieces are armour, or the ritualized after-image of such. Isn't one of the problems of bipedalism, among many, that it puts the male sexual organs somewhat at risk, as compared with their sensible hiding place on all fours?) The man hanging in agony from the ceiling in Bruegel's pen drawing *Justitia* repeats the pose of the humanoid bottom right in *Hermogenes*. Which is to say that the arrangement of limbs in question is perfectly possible in

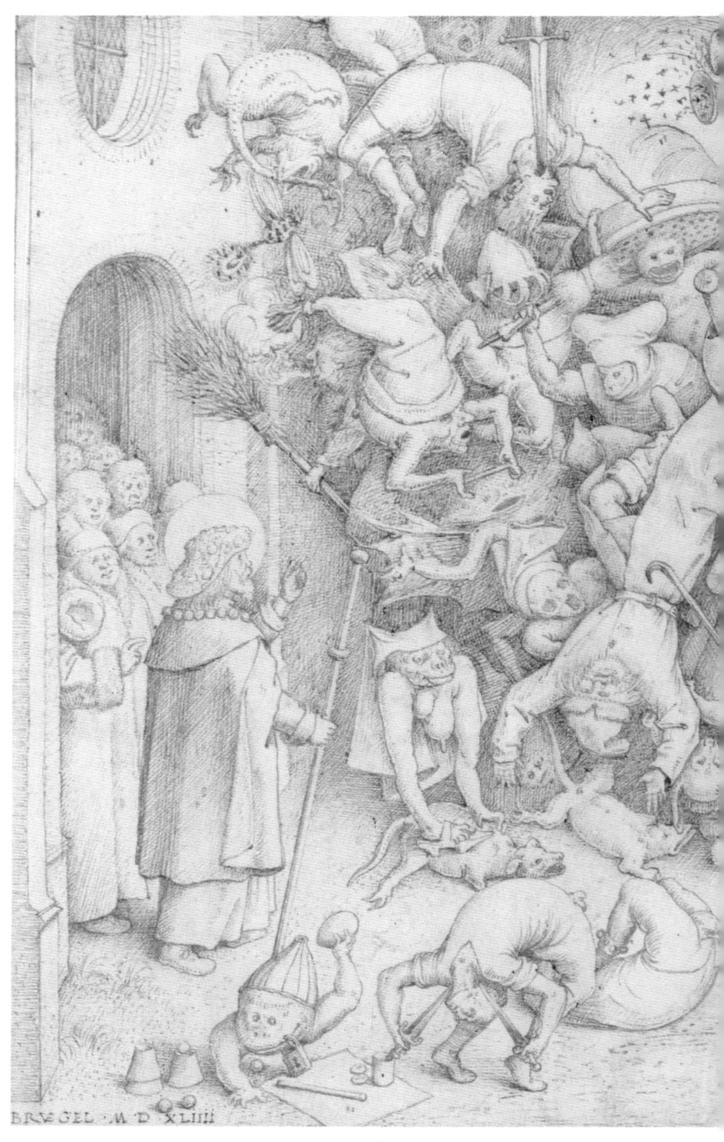

24. Pieter Bruegel the Elder, *The Fall of the Magician Hermogenes*, 1564, ink on paper

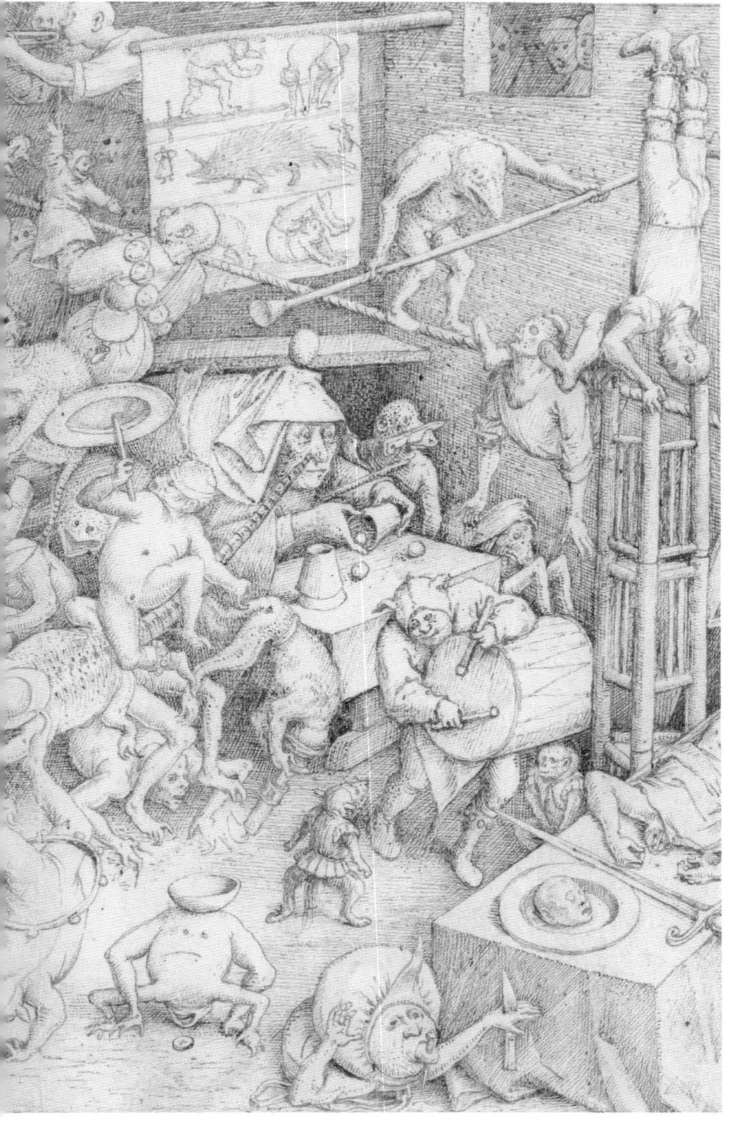

the real world, if men try hard enough. Again the codpiece is detailed. *The Cripples* remain unbearable for us, and no doubt were originally laughable, in particular because of the substitutes they have improvised for putting two feet on the ground. Speech they do not lack. If there is a question of their threatening our definition of the human or dancing at the edge of it, this cannot be because they lack language. They look to be talking too much.

Only Bruegel could have thought of putting his cripples on such tender, delicate, succulent grass. But why? What response did he mean to provoke?

We confront the question of Bruegel's ethics. *Justitia* and *The Cripples* put the question most mercilessly, but there are other late Bruegels almost as dreadful: *The Blind Leading the Blind*, for instance, or the *Two Monkeys*. The challenge for viewers of Bruegel has always been to understand how these visions of the frailty and cruelty of our nature could coexist with the immense humanity – the charity, the inclusive laughter, the compassion – of *Peasant Wedding* or the *Harvest*. Even *Cockaigne*, we have seen, is for some viewers a jeremiad.

Let us concede that the 'attitudes' of Bruegel's contemporaries to cases of agony and deformity, or even of unthinking callousness, were different from ours. Let us assume that the art historian Hessel Miedema is right when he tells us that sixteenth-century Netherlanders would have greeted the spectacle of leglessness with laughter.[40] 'Did people laugh?' he asks. 'Undoubtedly they did. They laughed above all at the bizarre, the deformed

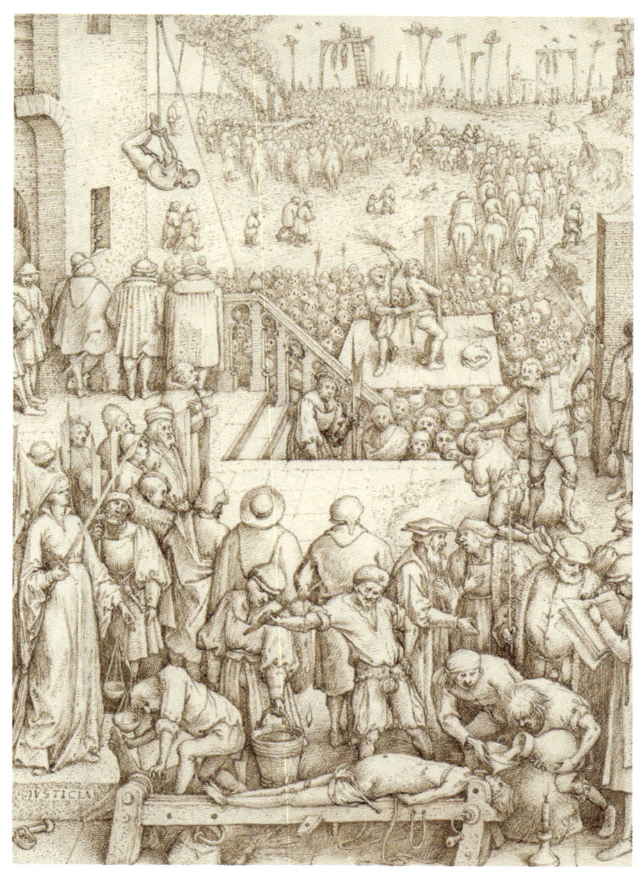

25. Pieter Bruegel the Elder, *Justitia*,
1559, detail, pen and brown ink on paper

and the weak.' I hear this laughter echoing in the spaces these pictures first occupied. And, equally, I hear the voice of the preacher, citing the obvious text. The blind leading the blind are no different from the rest of us. We are all falling.

Bruegel's pictures, in other words, issue from a world of derision and sanctimony. But that solves nothing. However hard a viewer may try to see Bruegel's actual visual preferences and strategies – his choices of scale, his particularization of expressions and movement, his set-up of spaces and ground plane, his turning of actors to face us or face away from us, and so on – *as* forms of dismissive laughter or moralization, it will always feel like forcing to do so. Why that is, exactly, is hard to pin down. It is not that the paintings in question are clearly at odds with their parent culture or intent on reversing that culture's terms. I doubt that even a phrase as anodyne as 'complicating the patron's frame of reference' is appropriate. What takes place, takes place in practice. When Bruegel comes to visualize his stock figures or stage his pieces of proverbial wisdom – making the figures fully present in a picture, setting them upright or lying them down, having them be 'idle' or 'crippled' or 'good for nothing' – the terms of understanding transmute.

And this is not because any sort of magic has been performed. Making anything in the world *particular*, taking advantage of the physical resources of the medium with that in mind, means that qualities and dimensions in the thing portrayed are taken seriously for the first time – aspects common wisdom ignores. But those aspects and dimensions are not (ever) invisible or non-existent in everyday life. They haunt the world of established truths and exclusions. People of all kinds – not just 'great artists', but people negotiating the ordinary ambiguities of the world – take advantage of this haunting, this latency. Life would be a self-destroying mechanism if they did not. Derision implies the possibility of pity, or sympathy, or common humanity. 'Blessed are the meek' is not so very distant from 'blessed are the outcast, the halt and the lame'. And even had this culture not possessed a set of canonical texts in which the Son of Man could be seen consorting with the wretched of the earth, or himself suffering the full blast of sadistic laughter, the culture would still not have been easy – unequivocal – in its contempt for and dehumanization of the weak or disabled. No culture can be: dehumanization is an activity, a feat (no doubt often performed effectively) that has in its bones a sense of what, in its object, the conjuration is directed against. All human vocabularies have a gradient that expresses this awareness; and especially a gradient that harps on the thinness of the line between the genuine ethical negative and its various counterfeits – between roaring anathema and frozen reproach, between pessimism and misanthropy or piety and sanctimoniousness, between moral judgment and cant. One man's blasphemer is another's early Christian martyr.

Bruegel seems specifically to have been interested in the fine line. His *Misanthrope* stands precisely on it: neither securely figure of fun nor hero of inner otherworldliness.

As usual the artist enlists the full ambiguity of the pro-verbial to put us, as readers and viewers, in a quandary. 'Om dat de werelt is soe ongetru / Daer om gha ic in den ru': 'Because the world is so untrue, I go about in mourn-ing.' It is unusual for the proverb to be written, as it is here, more or less in the picture space.[41] And does not the declaration have just a trace of ostentation to it? Could performing one's withdrawal from the world in this way – one's disappointment in it – end up as just one more performance among others? Are not the *pleurant*'s clasped hands and pursed lips a touch self-congratulatory? ('Hij schijt op de wereld.'[42] But even this Bruegel is capable of sympathizing with.) Bruegel's pictures are short on villains. Even the cutpurse World has his reasons: he wants to get out of those ragged trousers. The misanthrope's purse is too big, red and heavy. The analogous cripple in *Netherlandish Proverbs*, slipping inside a similar globe of glass, provides the proper apology: 'You have to slither if you want to get through the world.'[43]

How often the word *wereld* sounds out in Bruegel. Of all forms of speech, proverbs are the least afraid of totalizing: the world for them is as concrete a thing as a broom or a barrel or a gallows. In *Netherlandish Proverbs* the blind leading the blind exist at the farthest point of the proverbial universe portrayed: they are striding round a headland at the edge of the sea. The sun goes with them (but also the gallows across an estuary). They seem to be exiting towards the landscape of the *Fall of Icarus*. The proverb itself – 'When one blind man leads another, they both fall into a ditch' – applies here only lightly.

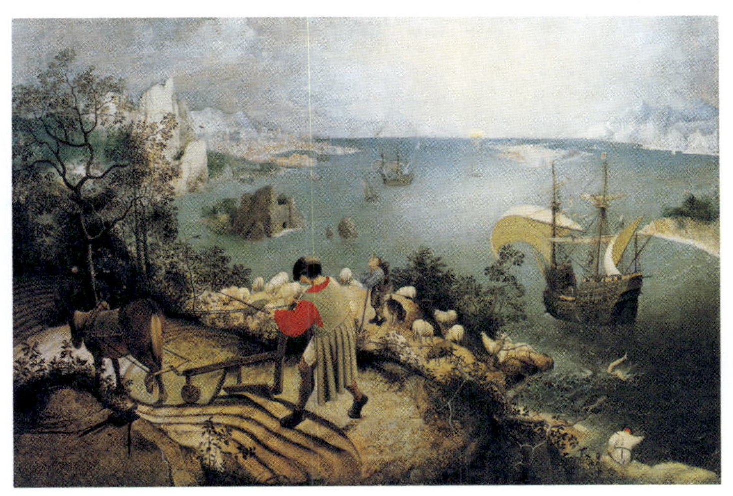

26. Pieter Bruegel the Elder,
The Fall of Icarus, c. 1555

I think that the full-scale painting of the blind men Bruegel did later set itself the task of *making* the proverb apply, literalizing it. But literalizing it – monumentalizing it, making the proverb loom up in the flesh in front of the viewer – also peeled it away from the proverbial frame. Proverbs are concrete but blessedly abbreviated: their fewness of words is the key to their power: they slip by or slip out almost before the user is aware of producing them. Stopping a proverb in its tracks, magnifying it, giving it specific features – this is always in a sense turning it into something else.

The *Land of Cockaigne*, I have been arguing, comes out of this proverbial world. And as with many a proverb, its tone is hard to catch. It is comic, certainly; it wears its wisdom and compassion lightly, and works to show us a world – a set of human and animal actors – that is absurd and wonderful at the same time: unbelievable and irresistible, just because (this seems to me the thought) that is the nature of the world in general. Some such proposal about humanity underlies all the best of Bruegel: he wants us to go on wondering at the juxtaposition, in his great *Magpie on the Gallows*, of a crude instrument of public death, taken for granted by those who have grown up with it, and an irrepressible urge to dance in its shadow.[44] I do not think the word 'callousness' will do to sum up the attitudes and forms of life in play here – Bruegel's and the dancers' – any more than 'peasant simple-mindedness' or 'sheer will to survive'. Something of these, no doubt; as well as unapologetic earthiness and openness (on the part of people who work the land) to the instigations of weather, light, the seasons.

That there are parallels between *Magpie on the Gallows* and the *Land of Cockaigne* is obvious. The peasant shitting in the corner of *Magpie* is partner to the man in *Cockaigne* pulling himself out of the gruel; *Magpie*'s beautiful centre foreground – the sunlit hummock supporting the gallows, with its animal skeleton and pecking bird – is *Cockaigne*'s tilting slope quieted down; the dancers in *Magpie* have made a small eternity for themselves, where death for a moment is in abeyance. But it would be wrong to press the analogies too far. *Magpie* is as close as we come in Bruegel to a comprehensive statement about the place of human sociability – the strange mixture of sadism and togetherness that seems intrinsic to it – in the whole order of the earth. It makes sense that the picture (if we are to believe an early biographer) is singled out in Bruegel's will as a bequest to his wife, apparently a special treasure. *Cockaigne*, by contrast, is the opposite of a panorama or 'world landscape'. It is imaginary – essentially a close-up. Paradise – an end to sadism *and* togetherness, it seems – can be posited only as something too near, too fat, too immobile to be true. I do not believe that Bruegel's picture is simply satirizing the Evangelist's 'no more death, neither sorrow, nor crying' – it looks to me full of wonder at the idea of escape from all three – but the last thing it asks us to do is assent to the vision or believe it a real possibility.

So how *is* the picture's amalgam of gravity and light-heartedness meant to be taken? What did Bruegel expect from viewers if not their assent? Here he is, the great pessimist, entertaining for once the idea of a life free from hunger and terror. But in what spirit?

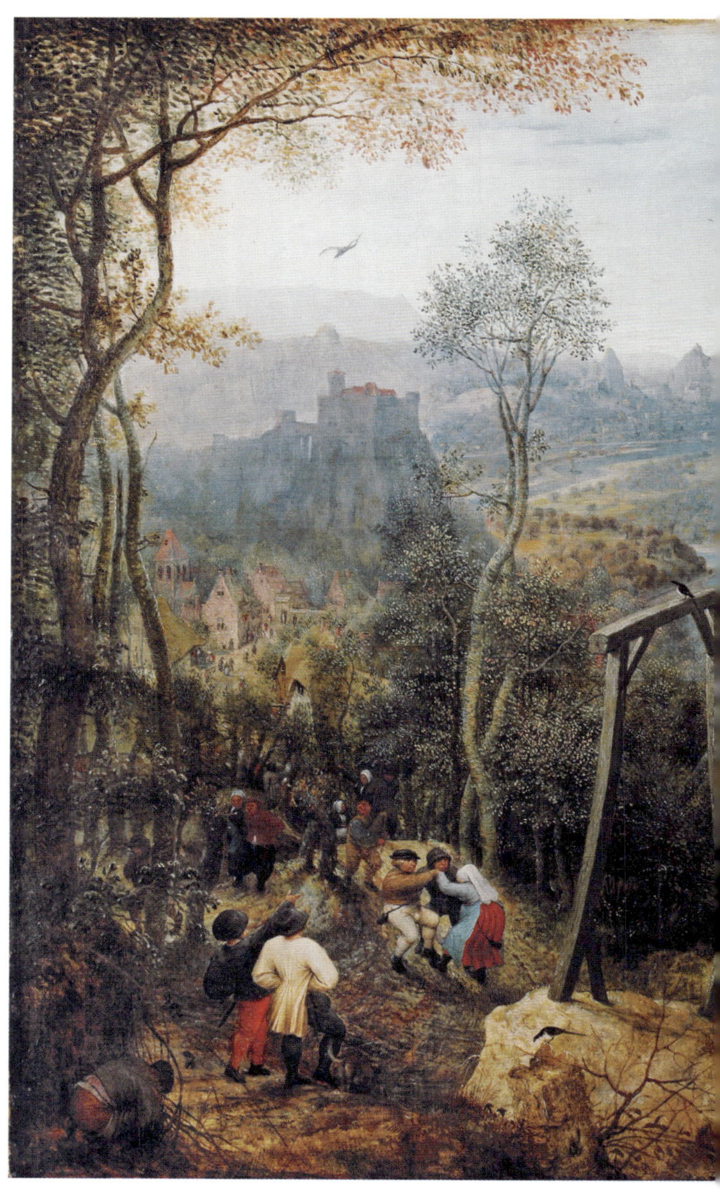

27. Pieter Bruegel the Elder, *Magpie on the Gallows*, 1568

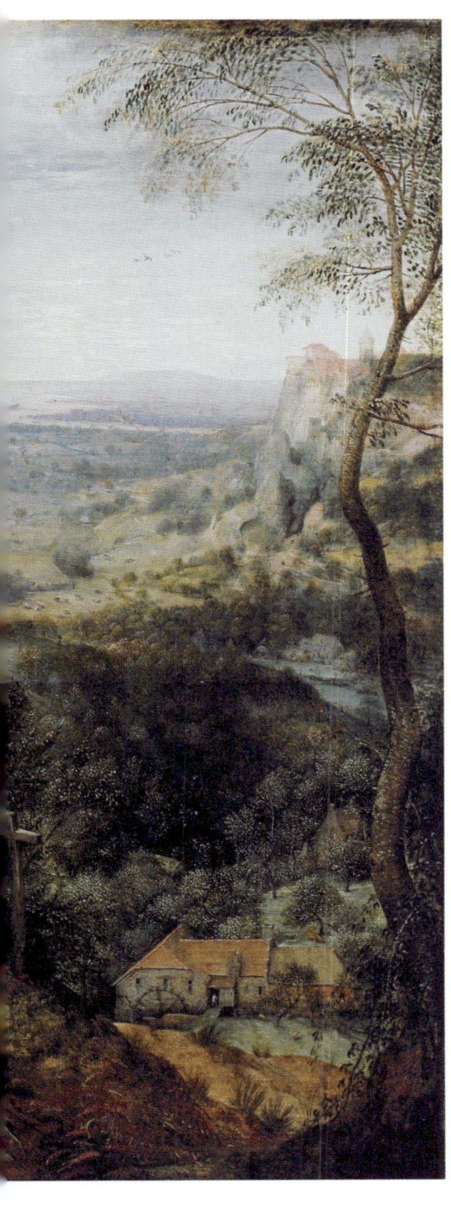

Such questions are sharpened – but only made more perplexing, I feel – if finally we try to confront the full meaning of the picture's date, written above Bruegel's name in capitals bottom left. There is no need for a full catalogue of horrors, but it bears repeating that 1567 was a fateful year – a turning point – in the revolt of the Netherlands against Spain, and that, as so often, religious differences focused and embittered the struggle. On 22 August 1567 the Duke of Alba arrived in Brussels at the head of a Spanish army, tasked with ending civil rebellion and liquidating Protestant heresy. On 5 September he set up his 'Council of Troubles'. Five years of bloodshed followed. Alba boasted later of having executed 18,000 Calvinists: an exaggeration, but pointing to the spectacle of cruelty – mass public executions, burnings, torture, shaming of women and maddening of children – that was an integral part of his campaign.[45] Monstrosities of this kind had not begun with Alba's invasion and did not stop when his army went south. Tens of thousands of Protestants (as far as numbers can be reconstituted) had been executed even before 1565; as many as 150,000 chose exile in the half-century following.[46] True or false, overblown or invented, scenes like the one I illustrate – from a Dutch print denouncing the Spaniards at the siege of Haarlem – are the *Land of Cockaigne*'s (and *Justitia*'s) proper accompaniment.

Through the decades, viewers of *Cockaigne* have sensed its nearness to such obscenities. Heaven on earth is hard to disentangle from hell. And this may be Bruegel's point: his *Cockaigne* speaks back to the murderous certainties

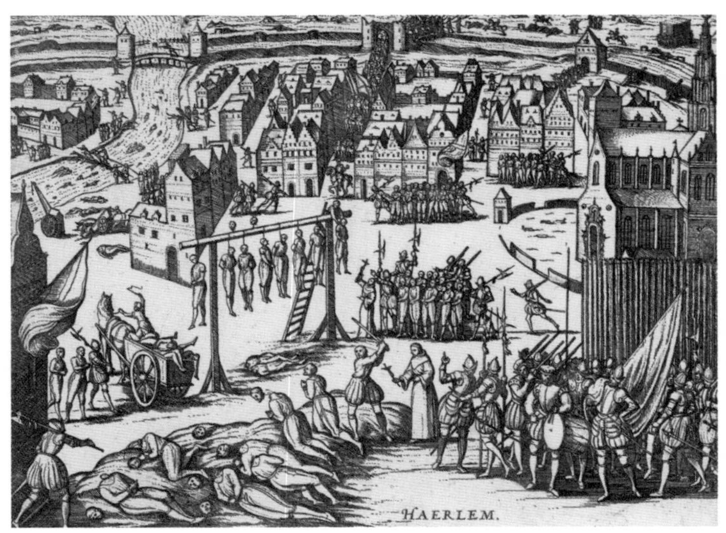

28. Anon, *Murder in Haarlem by the Spaniards, 1573*, 1573–75, detail, etching

in the city along the shore. It offers a model for thinking of alternative worlds – thinking them through, realizing them, dwelling on their substance and detail – without the thinker 'believing' in the thought as it comes into being … having the thought be shot through with a consciousness of its impossibility, maybe even absurdity … but not having the disbelief *invalidate* the thought … insisting quietly, on the contrary, that the thought keeps alive a necessary dream, a horizon of action and consciousness, an insubordination intrinsic to the human.

Of course, I have also been suggesting that Bruegel, in offering such a way of thinking in 1567 – maintaining the kind of balance he did between seriousness and unseriousness, even in the face of horror – had resources at his disposal that we now seem to lack, at least those of us living in the tranquillized 'West'. His unseriousness could tap naturally into a vein of insolence and down-to-earthness (and an unappeasable wish for escape) that ran deep in the culture of the European working masses. The nexus of wishes involved here, as far as we can understand it, was the opposite of a dead, generalized cynicism about 'power' or a fatalism posing as hardheadedness. Compare the mass culture we know.

Paradise may be fantastical in Bruegel, but nothing will convince me it is simply a delusion. The egg has emerged from the gully and steadies itself on splayed chicken legs. The grass slope beckons. The creature's pride in what it has to offer is immeasurable. Down one side of its shell runs the thin stream of yolk. The man coming out of the porridge will soon need feeding. The earth's great cycle begins again.

NOTES

1 See the most recent studies: Herman Pleij, *Dreaming of Cockaigne: Medieval Fantasies of the Perfect Life*, trans. Diane Webb (New York, 2001 [first Dutch edition 1997]), and Hilario Junior, *Cocagne: Histoire d'un pays imaginaire* (Paris, 2013 [first Brazilian edition 1998]).

2 See Jean Delumeau (ed.), *La mort des pays de Cocagne: Comportements collectifs de la Renaissance à l'âge classique* (Paris, 1976).

3 See Timothy Clark, 'Painting at Ground Level', in *The Tanner Lectures on Human Values*, vol. 24 (Salt Lake City, 2004), pp. 131–72.

4 Alfred Tennyson, 'Tithonus', in Christopher Ricks (ed.), *Tennyson: A Selected Edition* (Berkeley and Los Angeles, 1978), pp. 584, 992. (The word 'earth' is used in the first two versions of the poem; the third opts for 'field'.)

5 See Roger Marijnissen, *Bruegel: Tout l'oeuvre peint et dessiné* (Paris, 1988), pp. 242–43. (Marijnissen notes, with an irony that does not invalidate the judgment, that personnel and poses in *Spring* 'se prêtent à merveille à une exégèse marxiste'.)

6 Edward Snow, *Inside Bruegel: The Play of Images in Children's Games* (New York, 1997), p. 120. Snow's book, scrupulous in its representation of the art-historicist scholarship it is arguing with, devastating in its arguments and endlessly suggestive in its readings of Bruegel's imagery, is conspicuous by its absence from almost all recent art-historical literature.

7 For a judgment on Snow (as opposed to lofty silence), see Keith Moxey, 'Pieter Bruegel and Popular Culture', in David Freedberg, *The Prints of Pieter Bruegel the Elder* (Tokyo, 1989), pp. 45–46. Moxey gets Snow's point about the ambiguity of Bruegel's 'signifying structures' wrong. Snow's argument is that sixteenth-century culture itself (not 'the evidence' we have of it), insofar as we can reconstruct its full range, is ambiguous in its attitudes to and evaluation of childhood (as are most cultures). Compare sixteenth-century attitudes to the 'low', the 'earthy', the peasant and the 'folk'. On the accusation of undue subjectivity regularly levelled at Snow, see the always-to-be-reread 'Unfair Intimidation', in Theodor Adorno, *Minima Moralia*, trans. Edward Jephcott (London, 1974), pp. 69–70: 'The notions of subjective and objective have been completely reversed. Objective [now] means the non-controversial aspect of things, their unquestioned impression,

the façade made up of classified data, that is, the subjective; and they call subjective anything that breaches that façade, engages the specific experience of a matter, casts off ready-made judgments and substitutes relatedness to the object for the majority consensus of those who do not even look at it, let alone think about it – that is, the objective.'

8 From a large literature, see, for example, Moxey, 'Bruegel and Popular Culture', and Moxey, 'Sebald Beham's church anniversary holidays: festive peasants as an instrument of repressive humor', *Simiolus*, 12 (1982), pp. 107–30 (the clearest statement of Moxey's background assumptions). Compare Hans-Joachim Raupp, *Bauernsatiren: Entstehung und Entwicklung des bäuerlichen Genres in der deutschen und niederländischen Kunst ca. 1470–1570* (Niederzier, 1986); Margaret Sullivan, *Bruegel's Peasants: Art and Audience in the Northern Renaissance* (Cambridge, 1994); Ethan Matt Kavaler, *Pieter Bruegel: Parables of Order and Enterprise* (Cambridge, 1999). For contrary views, see Svetlana Alpers, 'Bruegel's Festive Peasants', *Simiolus*, 6 (1972–73), pp. 163–76; Margaret Carroll, 'Peasant Festivity and Political Identity in the Sixteenth Century', *Art History*, 10 (1987), pp. 289–314. The debate about Bruegel's peasants may now be escaping from this previous frame: see Stephanie Porras, *Pieter Bruegel's Historical Imagination* (University Park, PA, 2016); and Joseph Koerner, *Bosch and Bruegel: From Enemy Painting to Everyday Life* (Princeton and Oxford, 2016), especially pp. 13–20, 268–74.

9 Hans Sedlmayr, 'Bruegel's *Macchia*', trans. Frederic Schwartz, in Christopher Wood (ed.), *The Vienna School Reader: Politics and Art Historical Method in the 1930s* (New York, 2000), p. 336.

10 See Pleij, *Dreaming of Cockaigne, passim*; Junior, *Cocagne, passim*; Marijnissen, *Bruegel*, pp. 333–34 (citing a Dutch description of *Luye-leckerlandt* from 1546); Delumeau, *La mort du pays de Cocagne, passim*; and, from a large literature, Louis Lebeer, 'Le Pays de Cocagne (Het Luilekkerland)', *Musées Royaux des Beaux-Arts de Belgique, Bulletin*, 4 (1955), pp. 199–214, and Lebeer's entry on the *Cockaigne* print in *Catalogue raisonné des estampes de Pierre Bruegel l'Ancien* (Brussels, 1969); Jacques Le Goff, 'L'utopie mediévale: le pays de Cocagne', *Revue européenne des sciences sociales*, 27 (1989), pp. 271–86; and Hans Gilomen, 'Das Schlaraffenland und andere Utopien im Mittelalter', *Basler Zeitschrift für Geschichte und Altertumskunde*, 104 (2004), pp. 213–48.

11 Some of Junior's interpretations of the *fabliau* are unconvincing, but he establishes that the text plays on multiple and often enigmatic

registers: see Junior, *Cocagne*, pp. 25–78 and *passim*. On the oral basis of the legend, see Pleij, *Dreaming of Cockaigne*, pp. 3–4, 28; and Junior, *Cocagne*, pp. 18–19, 59–60, 76, discussing the uses made of it by different classes.

12 See Junior, *Cocagne*, pp. 312–30: pushing the argument too far, but pointing to an unmistakable evolution.

13 First reproduced in Ross Frank, 'An Interpretation of *Land of Cockaigne* (1567) by Pieter Bruegel the Elder', *Sixteenth Century Journal*, 22 (1991), p. 303.

14 See Pleij, *Dreaming of Cockaigne*, pp. 431, 434 (with the sentences cited below), and discussion on pp. 301–3. On the Free Spirit heresy, see R. Lerner, *The Heresy of the Free Spirit in the Later Middle Ages* (Berkeley, 1972); Cohn, *Pursuit of the Millennium*, pp. 148–86; Pleij, *Dreaming of Cockaigne*, pp. 311–34.

15 Quoted from Lebeer in the Brussels *Catalogue raisonné*, p. 156. See also Manfred Sellink's entry in Nadine Orenstein (ed.), *Pieter Bruegel, Drawings and Prints* (New York, 2001), pp. 256–57.

16 On Bruegel's inwardness with the calendar and key figures of Carnival, see Claude Gaignebet, 'Le combat de Carnaval et de Carême de P. Bruegel (1559)', *Annales: Economies, Sociétés, Civilisations*, 27 (1972), pp. 313–45.

17 See Pleij, *Dreaming of Cockaigne*, pp. 89–162 (the 'ritual surfeit' quote is on p. 130); and Junior, *Cocagne*, pp. 79–95, 312–13.

18 Max J. Friedländer, *Early Netherlandish Painting*, vol. 14 (Leyden and Brussels, 1976), p. 16.

19 Ibid., p. 34.

20 Ibid., p. 33.

21 For recent discussion of the Bosch–Bruegel relationship, see Tine Luk Meganck, *Pieter Bruegel the Elder, Fall of the Rebel Angels: Art, Knowledge and Politics on the Eve of the Dutch Revolt* (Milan and Brussels, 2014), pp. 35–63; and, pre-eminently, Koerner, *Bosch and Bruegel*, pp. 77–94 and *passim*. (The present chapter's view of the 'everyday', the allegorical and the theological in Bruegel ends up largely disagreeing with Koerner's. His culminating account of the Brussels *Winter Landscape with Bird Trap* is powerful, but my dissent from it can be summed up as follows: what seems to me most spellbinding about the bird trap in the scene is its ordinariness, its carefully plotted unobtrusiveness, its improvised homeliness, its integration into the picture's whole patterning of nature and culture. Koerner believes that the trap presents us with a 'terrifying perspective' on

the world. I'd like to know more about the contribution of pigeon pie to a Netherlander's winter diet.)

22 Early versions of the moralizing interpretation could be eloquent: see Louis Maeterlinck, *Le genre satirique dans la peinture flamande* (Ghent, 2nd edn 1907): 'The painter may have wished to satirize his fellow-countrymen, who were too ready to indulge in the pleasures of the table and idleness, and to show that – as coming events were to prove – an excessive preoccupation with physical well-being would undermine their moral courage and make them ready to accept oppression and tyranny', quoted in Piero Bianconi, *The Complete Paintings of Bruegel* (London, 1969), p. 108. By the time of Fritz Grossmann, *Bruegel: The Paintings* (London, 1966 [first published 1955]), p. 202, the picture 'is obviously intended as a condemnation of the sins of gluttony and sloth'; compare Kavaler, *Pieter Bruegel*, pp. 8–9 and no. 124, for a recent statement of the case; and Marijnissen, *Bruegel*, pp. 333–34, for a selection of arguments. Most art-historical treatments (not all) recognize that the picture was also meant to be funny.

23 For the Dutch text, see Freedberg, *Prints of Pieter Bruegel*, p. 169. I have preferred the translation in Marijnissen, *Bruegel*, p. 337.

24 See Sellink in Orenstein, *Bruegel, Drawings and Prints*, pp. 256–57, building on Stephen Kostyshyn, 'A Reintroduction to the Life and Work of Peeter Baltens', PhD dissertation, Case Western Reserve University (Cleveland, 1994). On the altarpiece, see Marijnissen, *Bruegel*, p. 11.

25 The question of Bruegel's relation to the 'Boschian' recurs; and *Cockaigne* may indeed be partly an answer to *The Garden of Earthly Delights*. By 1567 the *Garden* was a coveted trophy: it belonged to William of Orange, and in December 1567 was still on display in his Nassau palace. Tine Meganck, *Fall of the Rebel Angels*, pp. 41–48, 148–51, makes the case for Bruegel's earlier knowledge of William's triptych. *Cockaigne* reverses many of the *Garden*'s key terms: the chosen few are preferred to the multitude, closeness displaces panorama, gluttony trumps *voluptas*, and insensibility nude acrobatics.

26 Porras, *Pieter Bruegel's Historical Imagination*, pp. 49–50, sees *Cockaigne* as deliberately nostalgic in its picture of a world still organized around the 'three estates', for all the presence of a modern city – maybe even Antwerp – on the other side of the mountain.

27 Peter Sahlins, personal communication. The idea that *Cockaigne*, as well as other pictures from around 1567, in some sense responded to contemporary horrors begins fairly early in the literature. See, for example, René van Bastelaer and Georges Hulin de Loo, *Peter*

Bruegel l'Ancien, son oeuvre et son temps (Brussels, 1907), p. 134: 'Les premiers combats, les troubles et l'occupation d'Anvers par les troupes des Gueux, l'arrivée du duc d'Albe le 16 août, l'arrestation d'Egmont et de Horne, et l'érection du Conseil des troubles marquent l'année suivante, et, par ironie évidente, c'est le moment que Bruegel choisit pour executer sa peinture du Luilekkerland ... L'idée de peindre le Luilekkerland dans les circonstances présentes était ironique au suprême degré.' Frank, 'An Interpretation', the most thoroughgoing attempt to read *Cockaigne* as politically coded, is unconvincing: individual readings and claims are farfetched (for instance, most of the analogies made between *Cockaigne*'s imagery and proverbs), and the argument as a whole built on non sequiturs. David Kunzle, 'Spanish Herod, Dutch Innocents: Bruegel's *Massacres of the Innocents* in their sixteenth-century political contexts', *Art History*, 24 (February 2001), pp. 51–82, seems to me the most scrupulous recent discussion of politics in Bruegel's late work: he makes a case for contemporary allusion in the *Massacre* and *Census in Bethlehem*, as well as the *Conversion of Saint Paul*, *Sermon of Saint John the Baptist* and perhaps even *Magpie on the Gallows*, but passes over Frank's reading of *Cockaigne* in charitable silence.

28 Collect, Fourth Sunday after Epiphany.

29 See Friedländer, *Early Netherlandish Painting*, p. 37: 'Since the body, in function and configuration, determined the fall of drapery, it was deemed urgent and indispensable to acquire an intimate knowledge of the organism in its cocoon. Only Bruegel took in the appearance as a whole ... He rejoiced in its many manifestations. There was but one body, but many forms of dress and countless silhouettes adopted by the moving body in its swathings.'

30 On Bruegel's relation to the world of proverbs, see especially David Kunzle, 'Bruegel's Proverb Painting and the World Upside Down', *Art Bulletin*, 59 (June 1977), pp. 197–202; Alan Dundes and Claudia Stibbe, *The Art of Mixing Metaphors: A Folkloristic Interpretation of the 'Netherlandish Proverbs' by Pieter Bruegel the Elder* (Helsinki, 1981); Rainald Grosshans, *Pieter Bruegel d. Ä: Die niederländischen Sprichwörter* (Berlin, 2003), pp. 20–31; and Margaret Carroll, *Painting and Politics in Northern Europe: Van Eyck, Bruegel, Rubens, and their Contemporaries* (University Park, PA, 2008), pp. 33–46.

31 How much or what kind of 'folly' the tower may be is a question the Vienna picture leaves open. As a feat of building Babel is lovingly described. Compare, for a reading inspired by Hegel's rewriting of the

story of the tower in his *Lectures on Aesthetics*, Catharina Kahane, 'Der Fall Babel. Volksbildung im Pieter Bruegels d. Ä Turmbau', in Beate Fricke et al. (eds.), *Bilder und Gemeinschaften* (Munich, 2010), pp. 141–68.

32 For arguments about cooking and civilization, see Claude Lévi-Strauss, *The Raw and the Cooked*, trans. John and Doreen Weightman (London, 1970); Marcel Detienne and Jean-Pierre Vernant, *The Cuisine of Sacrifice among the Greeks*, trans. Paula Wissing (Chicago, 1989); and compare Walter Burkert, *Homo Necans: The Anthropology of Ancient Greek Sacrificial Ritual and Myth*, trans. Peter Bing (Berkeley and Los Angeles, 1983).

33 Genesis 3: 19.

34 From the more recent literature, see Walter Gibson, *Peter Bruegel the Elder: Two Studies* (Lawrence, KS, 1991), pp. 53–86. Compare the typical verdict in Grossmann, *Bruegel: The Paintings*, p. 192: 'It is the idea of Last Judgment closely connected with death which for Bruegel the Christian makes physical death so frightening.'

35 On this topic see Pleij, *Dreaming of Cockaigne*, pp. 165–81, 191–206, 281–97 (this last section pointing to the possibility that Cockaigne and *Luilekkerland* sometimes consciously poked fun at ideas of paradise).

36 Svetlana Alpers, oral response to my 'Painting at Ground Level' lectures, Princeton University, 2002.

37 See *The Catholic Encyclopedia*, ed. Charles Herbermann et al. (New York, 1912), vol. 13, p. 551.

38 From the large literature, see Fernand Braudel, *Capitalism and Material Life 1400–1800*, trans. Miriam Kochan (New York, 1973); Neil McKendrick et al., *The Birth of a Consumer Society: The Commercialization of Eighteenth-Century England* (London, 1982); Ben Fine and Ellen Leopold, *The World of Consumption* (London and New York, 1993); John Brewer and Roy Porter (eds.), *Consumption and the World of Goods* (London, 1993).

39 The art-historical literature – for instance, the majority of items indicated in note 9 – presents us with a Bruegel whose art equivocated constantly between moral disapproval of the excesses and naiveties it showed and nostalgia for the simplicities of a vanishing 'folk'. It is true that some such mixture of censure and sentimentality soon became a standard ingredient of modern consciousness: whether Bruegel pioneered it remains questionable.

40 Hessel Miedema, 'Realism and comic mode: the peasant', *Simiolus*, 9 (1977), pp. 205–19; the quoted passage is on p. 211. Compare on the

same page: 'If I am correct about this, it is out of the question that anyone of erudition (and erudition is something that Bruegel and print publishers clearly had in abundance) could ever have laughed uninhibitedly at peasant scenes in Bruegel's day.' For less joyless views of Bruegel's world, see Johan Verberckmoes, *Laughter, Jestbooks and Society in the Spanish Netherlands* (Basingstoke, 1999); and Walter Gibson, *Pieter Bruegel and the Art of Laughter* (Berkeley and Los Angeles, 2006).

41 Scholars have doubted that the words were present in the picture originally, though it seems that the picture made room for some such inscription: see Koerner, *Bosch and Bruegel*, p. 26.

42 'I shit on the world': a saying illustrated in Bruegel's *Netherlandish Proverbs*.

43 See discussion in Wilhelm Fraenger, *Das Bild der 'Niederländischen Sprichwörter' – Pieter Bruegels verkehrte Welt* (Amsterdam, 1999 [first published 1923]), p. 48. The verb *krommen* resists translation: 'stoop' or even 'grovel' are possible renderings.

44 Compare Koerner, *Bosch and Bruegel*, pp. 355–64, for a reading of *Magpie* that sees the picture as belonging to a cluster of works that respond to Alba's reign of terror – even reflecting a new consciousness of the gallows' (the Law's) arbitrariness. I feel the painting's overall atmosphere distinguishes it from the grimmer, bleaker, more 'polit-ical' works immediately preceding it, in which soldiers, and wintry barrenness, stand for the reality of present power.

45 See Kunzle, 'Spanish Herod', pp. 53–54, for a good brief survey. Numbers vary wildly; perceptions trumped statistics. Jonathan Israel, *The Dutch Republic: Its Rise, Greatness, and Fall* (Oxford, 1995), pp. 159–60, puts the number of executions under Alba at 'more than 5,000'. Contemporaries seem to have believed the figure, for the whole period of conflict, to be six or even ten times as large.

46 Henri Pirenne, *Histoire de Belgique* (Brussels, 1922), vol. 3, p. 428, cited by Kunzle, 'Spanish Herod', p. 53.

LIST OF ILLUSTRATIONS

Measurements are given height before width, cm followed by inches

1. Pieter Bruegel the Elder, *Peasant Wedding,* 1568, detail. Oil on panel, 113 × 164 (44½ × 64½). Kunsthistorisches Museum Wien, Gemäldegalerie (Gemäldegalerie, 1027). **2.** Pieter Bruegel the Elder, *Land of Cockaigne,* 1567. Oil on panel, 51.5 × 78.3 (20¼ × 30⅞). Bayerische Staatsgemaldesammlungen – Alte Pinakothek München (8940). **3.** Pieter Bruegel the Elder, *Peasant Wedding,* 1568. Oil on panel, 113 × 164 (44½ × 64½). Kunsthistorisches Museum Wien, Gemäldegalerie (Gemäldegalerie, 1027). **4.** Pieter Bruegel the Elder, *The Triumph of Death,* 1562–63, detail. Oil on panel, 117 × 162 (46 × 63¾). Museo Nacional del Prado (P001393). **5.** Pieter Bruegel the Elder, *Spring,* 1565. Pen and ink on paper, 22.2 × 29 (8¾ × 11⅜). The Albertina Museum, Vienna (23750). **6.** Pieter Bruegel the Elder, *Children's Games,* 1560, detail. Oil on panel, 116.4 × 160.3 (45⅞ × 63⅛). Kunsthistorisches Museum Vienna, Gemäldegalerie. Photo Remo Bardazzi/Electa/Mondadori Portfolio/Getty Images. **7.** Anon, *Das gelobte abgebildete Schlaraffen-Land,* c. 1500–99. Woodcut, 63.4 × 101 (24¹⁵⁄₁₆ × 39¾). The Miriam and Ira D. Wallach Division of Art, Prints and Photographs: Print Collection, The New York Public Library (94885). **8.** Pieter van der Heyden, after Pieter Bruegel the Elder, *Fat Kitchen,* 1563. Engraving, 26.1 × 33.6 (10¼ × 13¼). Harris Brisbane Dick Fund, 1928. The Metropolitan Museum of Art (28.4(12)). **9.** Pieter van der Heyden, after Pieter Bruegel the Elder, *Big Fish Eat Little Fish,* 1557. Engraving, 23 × 29.6 (9 × 11⅝). Albertina, Vienna (DG1955/116). **10.** Pieter Bruegel the Elder, *Two Monkeys,* 1562. Oil on panel, 19.9 × 23.3 (7⅞ × 9⅛). Staatliche Museen zu Berlin, Gemäldegalerie / Christoph Schmidt (Gemäldegalerie, 2077). **11.** Pieter van der Heyden, attrib, after Pieter Bruegel the Elder, *Land of Cockaigne,* after 1570. Engraving, 20.8 × 27.9 (8¼ × 11). Harris Brisbane Dick Fund, 1926. The Metropolitan Museum of Art (26.72.44). **12.** Pieter Bruegel the Elder, *The Blind Leading the Blind,* 1568. Tempera on canvas, 86 × 154 (34 × 61). Museo e Real Bosco di Capodimonte, Naples. **13.** Pieter Bruegel the Elder, *Sea Battle off Naples,* 1563. Oil on panel, 42.2 × 71.2 (16⅝ × 28). Galleria Doria Pamphilj (FC 546). **14.** Pieter Bruegel the Elder, *The Cripples,* 1568. Oil on panel, 185 × 215 (72⅞ × 84⅝). Musée du Louvre, Département des Peintures (RF 730). **15.** Peeter Baltens, *Land of Cockaigne,* 1560s (after 1567?), detail. Engraving. Royal Library of Belgium.

ALSO AVAILABLE IN THE POCKET PERSPECTIVES SERIES:

Julian Bell on Painting

John Boardman on The Parthenon

E.H. Gombrich on Fresco Painting

James Hall on The Self-Portrait

Lucy Lippard on Pop Art

Linda Nochlin on The Body

Griselda Pollock on Gauguin

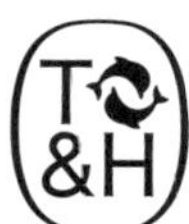

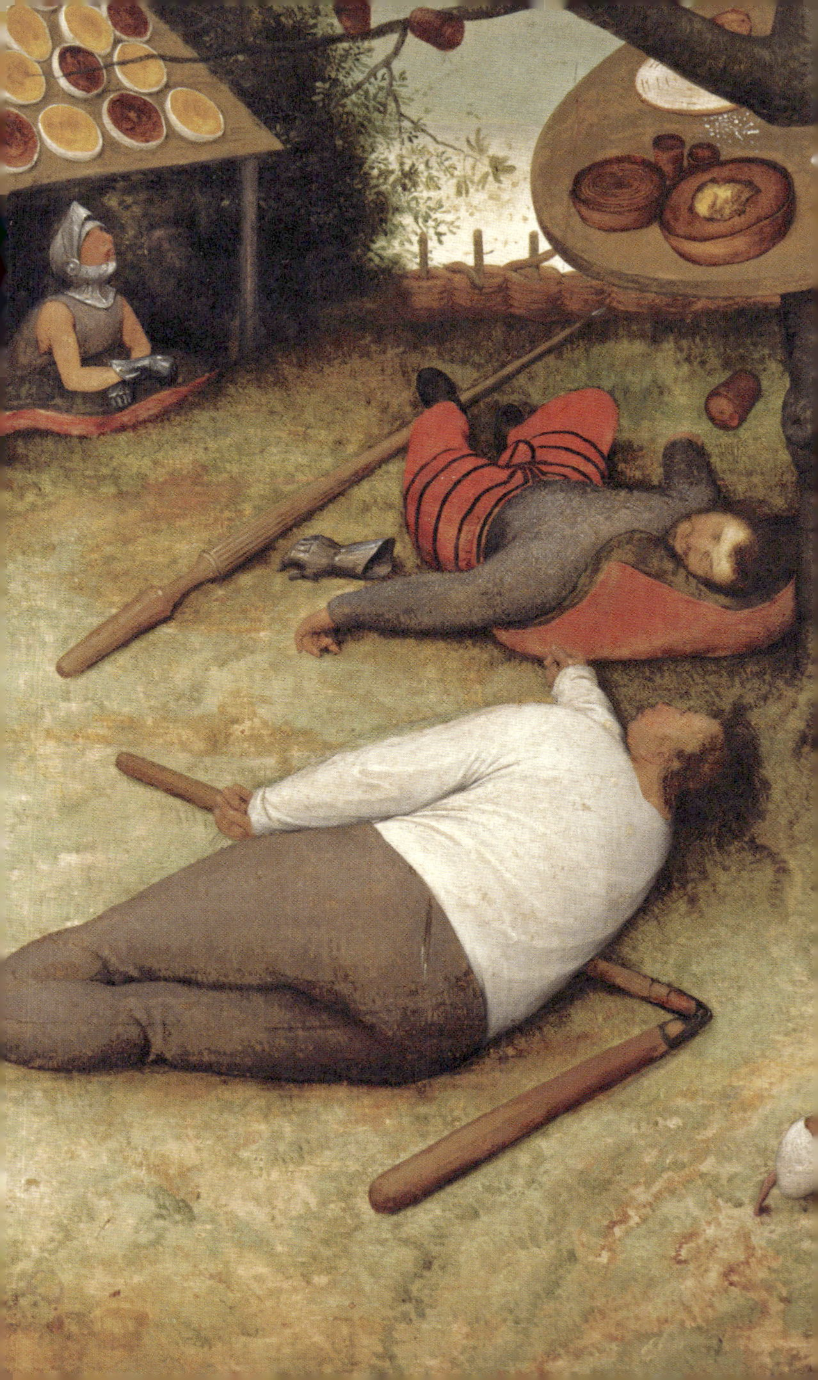